Nature Walks
near Philadelphia

NATURE WALKS
NEAR PHILADELPHIA

An AMC Nature Walks Book

SCOTT AND LINDA SHALAWAY

APPALACHIAN MOUNTAIN CLUB BOOKS
BOSTON, MASSACHUSETTS

Koen 12.95

Cover Photograph: *Tiger swallowtail*, Hal Korber
All photographs by the authors unless otherwise noted.
Cover Design: Elisabeth Leydon Brady
Book and Map Design: Carol Bast Tyler
Pencil drawings: Rudy Miller

Distributed by the Globe Pequot Press, Inc., Old Saybrook, CT

Published by the Appalachian Mountain Club. No part of this publication may be reproduced or transmitted in any form or by any
means, electronic or mechanical, including photocopying and record-
ing, or by any information storage or retrieval system, except as may
by expressly permitted by the 1976 Copyright Act or in writing from
the publisher. Requests for permission should be addressed in writing to Appalachian Mountain Club Books, 5 Joy Street, Boston, MA
02108.

Library of Congress Cataloging-in-Publication Data
Shalaway, Scott
    Nature walks near Philadelphia / Scott and Linda Shalaway.
        p.   cm.
    Includes index.
    ISBN 1-878239-52-X (alk. paper)
    1. Walking—Pennsylvania—Philadelphia Metropolitan Area—
Guidebooks.   2. Nature study—Pennsylvania—Philadelphia
Metropolitan Area—Guidebooks. 3. Philadelphia Metropolitan Area
(Pa.)—Guidebooks. I. Shalaway, Linda. II. Appalachian Mountain
Club. III. Title.
GV199.42.P42P546   1996
796.5'1'09748—dc20
                                                    96-30852
                                                        CIP
The paper used in this publication meets the minimum requirements
of the American National Standard for Information Sciences—
Permanence of Paper for Printed Library Materials, ANSI
Z39.48–1984.∞

**Due to changes in conditions,
use of the information in this book
is at the sole risk of the user.**

Printed on recycled paper using soy-based inks.
Printed in the United States of America.

10 9 8 7 6 5 4 3 2 1   97 98 99 00 01 02

Contents

Delaware County

Chester County

Berks County

Lancaster County

New Jersey

Delaware

PART 2: OVERNIGHTERS (MORE THAN 100 MILES)

Pike County

Nature Essays

We dedicate this book to Nora and Emma,
whose companionship and curiosity
enliven our walks, hikes, and lives.

Acknowledgments

For their support and enthusiasm, we thank our daughters, Nora and Emma. For their patience and assistance, we thank AMC editor Gordon Hardy and his staff. For darkroom help, we thank Kristin Gilmore and Art Limann. And for preserving and maintaining these special nature areas, we thank the many people who work at the places described in this book.

Introduction

If the millions of people who live in the greater Philadelphia area are typical Americans, most have at least a passing interest in nature. They enjoy nature programs on television. They will stop to admire a hummingbird sipping nectar from a bright red bee balm blossom. And they certainly enjoy watching a flock of bright red cardinals on a cold winter day.

Most of their wildlife watching, however, is passive. They might notice it while doing something else or watch it secondhand via television. Rarely do they get outdoors just to enjoy and marvel at the wonders of nature. This book is an attempt to change that.

We recognize that most city and suburban folks are just too busy with jobs, school, kids, and other family responsibilities; they simply have no time to sit down and plan a nature outing. We've tried to do that for you.

As you peruse these pages, we will introduce you to thirty-two places near Philadelphia where you can enjoy the peace and quiet of nature. Most are within an hour of the city, but a few require a longer drive and perhaps an overnight stay. Ricketts Glen, for example, is three hours from Philadelphia, but we consider it Pennsylvania's most spectacular natural feature. We had to include it. The Delaware Water Gap, just a few hours north of the city, offers nature at its best. Few would guess that such spectacular waterfalls can be found so close to the city.

The John Heinz National Wildlife Refuge, on the other hand, is just a stone's throw from Philadelphia International Airport, and Hawk Mountain is little more than an hour away.

We also included a few sites from south Jersey and one from Delaware. Having both grown up in Montgomery County, we know that many people vacation on the Jersey shore and that the Delaware Valley includes the tristate area.

We have purposefully excluded many potential sites within the city limits such as Fairmount Park and the Philadelphia Zoo for two reasons. First, we want to get city folks out of the city and into the country. Second, we suspect that luring suburbanites to the city for a nature walk would be a hard sell at best.

Though we recommend every place included in the book, we have our favorites. Cape May in May or early June, Hawk Mountain in October, and Ricketts Glen anytime are places we've visited dozens of times. We've never been disappointed. But all of the places we've included can be magical on an early morning walk or brisk fall autumn afternoon. The secret is to walk slowly, walk quietly, and use all five senses.

Our hope is that anyone interested in exploring natural areas near Philadelphia will choose this book to guide them. We describe what you can expect at each sight and sometimes take you by the hand as we walk a trail or two. We explain what we've seen at each spot, not to promise you the same experience but rather to give you an idea of what you might expect. Along the way, we've offered many tidbits of natural history. Scott's eight natural history essays sprinkled through the book bridge the gap between beginner and expert. You'll learn, for example, how some acorns actually avoid being eaten by squirrels and why the great horned owl is justly considered "king of the woods."

Read this book before you visit these places, and you'll know what to expect and how to get there. Take it along, and we'll help you understand what you see and hear.

Using this book requires no special knowledge. In fact, we wrote it with beginners in mind. The biggest obstacle to enjoying nature is getting out of the house and into the field. If we can tempt you to visit just a few of these spots, we will have succeeded. The contents of this book briefly introduce birds, wildflowers, and other watchable wildlife. Reinforce our tales with your own personal experiences, and you will be on the road to outdoor adventure. Who knows where it will take you— bird-watching, leaf peeping, camping, mountain biking, canoeing, or whitewater rafting?

Our mission is to get you outdoors. We think you'll find life on the wild side an irresistible pleasure.

To maximize the pleasure of your outdoor junkets, here are a few tips to help you avoid some of the problems many first time ramblers face:

- Upon arrival, always get a current map to the area you are about to explore. This will keep you abreast of any changes since we visited the area. If you find outdoor adventure appealing, buy a copy of DeLorme's *Pennsylvania Gazetteer*. This collection of detailed area maps is the best offered anywhere.

- Always let someone know where you plan to be— just in case.

- Always carry water in an unbreakable container.

- Always carry binoculars. That red spot high in the trees may be a scarlet tanager.

- If you are particularly interested in wildflowers, birds, butterflies, or trees, carry an appropriate field guide.

- Take your time and enjoy the drive to and from your destination. Pennsylvania's countryside is spectacular, some of the most beautiful in the nation.

- *Never* feed, touch, or pet a wild animal. If an animal seems "friendly," it is probably sick, maybe rabid.

- Wear sturdy shoes.

- When it's cold, dress in layers.

- Try a winter outing. You will find far fewer people, better vistas without vegetation obscuring the view, and no biting insects.

- Try visiting an area in four different seasons and have four completely different experiences—spring wildflowers, migrating spring and fall birds, winter waterfowl, summer reptiles and amphibians. Birding may be best in the spring, but wildflower and butterfly watching continue from spring through fall.

One final word of warning—deer ticks carry Lyme disease and are found throughout the area this book covers. Whether you're hiking, fishing, birding, or just playing baseball in the park, you might encounter deer ticks. They are much smaller than dog or wood ticks and are easy to overlook. An adult deer tick is about the size of this capital "O." A larval deer tick can be as small as the period at the end of this sentence.

The disease itself is caused by a bacterium that circulates in the blood of deer, rodents, and other mammals. The tick is merely the agent of transmission. Symptoms of Lyme disease may appear anywhere from days to years after a bite. This is one of the problems that make diagnosis difficult. Early on, a red rash may appear near the bite site. It may grow in size, or it may spread to other parts of the body. It may be round, or it may be irregularly shaped. It may last for a few days or as long as a month. It may be painless, or it may hurt or itch. Other early symptoms include nausea, chills, low-grade fever, fatigue, headaches, and achy joints and muscles. Untreated, Lyme disease can lead to serious neurological or cardiac disorders.

Lyme disease can now be confirmed with a blood test and treated with antibiotics. However, it can take eight weeks for antibodies to show up in the bloodstream, so a test done shortly after a bite can be falsely negative.

Clearly, Lyme disease is serious. More important, though, it's preventable. When you go outdoors in the spring and summer, do your best to make yourself tick-proof:

- Wear long sleeves and pants.
- Tuck pant legs into socks and keep shirt tucked in.
- Wrap duct tape around the pant leg/sock union.
- Wear light-colored clothing to make finding ticks easier.
- Spray clothes and exposed skin with a repellent containing DEET (avoid lips and eyes).

- Stay on trails and out of high grass.
- Check frequently for ticks while afield.
- Check every body fold and crevice thoroughly for ticks at day's end. (This is best done with a spouse or close friend).

If you find an attached tick, remove it by grabbing its head as close to the skin as possible with fine-tipped tweezers and pulling it out slowly. Don't burn the tick with a match or squeeze its body. These techniques can inject more tick fluid into you, and that's what you want to avoid.

The risk of Lyme disease is low, but increasing. By taking just a few simple precautions, you can reduce the risk to near zero.

Use common sense, be safe, and enjoy Pennsylvania's wild side.

Walk Locations

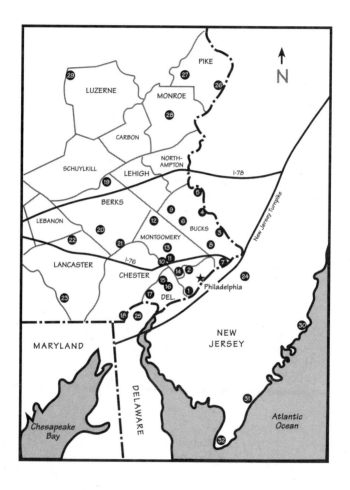

Part 1

—

Day Trips
(less than 100 miles)

Philadelphia County

1. John Heinz National Wildlife Refuge at Tinicum
Philadelphia

Hours: Daily, 8:00 A.M. to sunset

Tinicum Marsh's claim to fame is that it is **Pennsylvania's largest remaining freshwater tidal wetland**. More than 100 miles from the salt water of the Delaware Bay, Darby Creek flows into the Delaware River and is still subject to the bay's tidal influence. The twice daily tidal ebb and flow help make this wetland particularly rich in species diversity. More than 280 species of birds have been recorded here and more than 85 species nest here.

To some, Tinicum's cultural history is as rich and fascinating as its natural history. The original marsh, which measured some 5,700 acres, was settled, diked, and drained by Swedish, Dutch, and English settlers in 1634. By the end of World War I, urban development of the Philadelphia area left only about 200 acres of marsh.

In 1952 the Delaware Valley Ornithological Club proposed to Philadelphia mayor Joseph Clark Jr. that the city establish a municipal wildlife refuge. Clark responded, and in 1955 the Gulf Oil Corporation donated the property to Philadelphia. The city named the 145-acre parcel the Tinicum Wildlife Preserve.

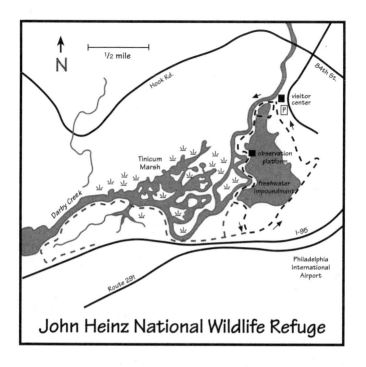

John Heinz National Wildlife Refuge

In the late 1960s construction of I-95 threatened the area, but local conservationists and congressmen convinced the Department of Interior to add it to the National Wildlife Refuge System. In 1971 Congress acquired the area and established the Tinicum National Environmental Center.

The refuge now covers nearly 1,000 acres. In 1991 it was renamed to honor Senator John Heinz, who helped preserve the Tinicum Marsh and died nearby in a tragic mid-air crash.

More than 8 miles of walking trails wind their way through the Tinicum Marsh. The walk we recommend follows a dike that separates a large freshwater impoundment from the adjacent tidal marsh. The marsh stretches beyond Darby Creek on the right; the freshwater pool is on the left. If you have a few hours, circle the impoundment at a leisurely pace.

Along the way, be sure to spend some time surveying the area from the elevated observation platform. With the city and the airport looming in the background, the significance of this urban wild area is inescapable. It's hard to believe that populations of ducks, rails, herons, egrets, frogs, turtles, muskrats, opossums, and deer thrive so close to a booming metropolis. It offers hopes that urban development and natural values need not be mutually exclusive, as long as community leaders are wise enough to protect sensitive natural areas in perpetuity.

If time is short (perhaps you're stopping by before catching a late-morning flight out of Philadelphia), take the boardwalk across the impoundment just a few hundred yards into the walk. Cross the water slowly, and watch for movement. You may see a water snake grab a frog or a muskrat swim silently from one patch of reeds to another. In May and June the vegetation teems with breeding birds. **Least bitterns, black-crowned night herons, and five species of rails** are just a few of the water birds known to nest in the area.

Wood ducks, arguably the most beautiful bird in North America, use the large nest boxes scattered around the marsh. Both male and female wood ducks are crested, but the males' colorful plumage screams for attention. Look for the orange bill, red ring around the eyes, and iridescent body colors. Though the hen is duller, her distinctive teardrop-shaped eye patch is diagnostic. Wood duck nest boxes are often placed directly over water to discourage predators such as raccoons, opossums, and rat snakes. Look for hens and their broods in June.

Three other marsh-loving songbirds can usually be found nesting in the vegetation circling the freshwater pool. Red-winged blackbirds are the most conspicuous. Males defend small territories and usually maintain pair bonds with several females. The streaky brown females are shy, inconspicuous, and easy to overlook. But singing males displaying their bright red shoulder patches are brilliantly visible. Even beginners will have no trouble recognizing the red-wing's song, a discordant "Kong-ka-reee!"

A flash of yellow and a loud series of triple notes—"Witchity, witchity, witchity"—means a common yellowthroat is nearby. This small warbler often cocks its tail like a wren when perched. Breeding males are easily recognized by the bright yellow throat and broad black mask that marks the face.

Our favorite Tinicum bird is uncommon across much of its range, but it's easy to find during a May or June visit to the marsh. **Marsh wrens** are secretive small brown birds that love to play peekaboo with birders. One moment they sing from the top of a cattail, the next they're hidden among the dense stand of stems. Look for a white eye line, a chestnut body, and a black back marked with white streaks. When you spot one, follow it closely with your binoculars. It may lead you to its nest, a football-shaped mass of vegetation with a side

Kids of all ages enjoy nature walks.

entrance. Typically the nest is anchored to the stems of reeds or cattails a foot or so above water level. Even if you didn't catch a glimpse of a marsh wren, you are certain to hear it. Its loud, rapid, liquid song is difficult to describe, but once you hear it, you'll always associate the sound with marshy areas.

When you return to the parking lot, check the visitor contact station for upcoming activities. You might want to return for a more organized walk with a naturalist.

Even busy travelers can take advantage of Tinicum's attractions. Scott flies in and out of Philadelphia several times a year on business, and he always plans a late-morning departure so he can spend an hour or two at the marsh before he returns his rental car.

Getting There

From I-95, take Exit 10 for the Philadelphia International Airport and Rte. 291. Take Rte. 291 east 0.7 mile to the intersection of 84th Street. Turn left onto 84th Street and continue 0.7 mile to Lindbergh Boulevard. Turn left onto Lindbergh and travel 0.25 mile to the refuge entrance. Follow signs to the parking area.

Facilities: A visitor contact station is open daily from 9:00 A.M. to 4:00 P.M. Portable toilets are available.

Best Time to Visit: April, May, June.

For More Information: Refuge Manager, John Heinz National Wildlife Refuge at Tinicum, 86th Street & Lindbergh Avenue, Philadelphia, PA 19153, or call 215-365-3118; or Refuge Headquarters, Suite 104, Scott Plaza II, Philadelphia, PA 19113, or call 215-521-0662.

Nearby Attractions: Philadelphia Zoo, Philadelphia Academy of Natural Science, New Jersey State Aquarium in Camden.

2. Schuylkill Center for Environmental Education
Philadelphia

Hours: 8:30 A.M. to 5:00 P.M. Sundays from 1:00 to 5:00 P.M. During August, closed on Sundays.

The Schuylkill Center is a **500-acre oasis** in the midst of one of the country's most densely populated regions. Fields, woodlands, ponds, streams, and thickets offer the illusion of remoteness, an illusion interrupted only by the spectacular view of center city from the Upper Fields Trail.

We recommend the Schuylkill Center for adults and children alike. Nine interconnecting hiking trails, none longer than a mile, combine for a total of 6 miles. The paved Widener Trail provides wheelchair access through fields and forest and past Shadow Pond.

Our girls had fun designing a customized hike. Using the trail guide, they started us out on the Upper Fields Trail, which begins behind the visitor center. The trail crosses an old field, and through breaks in the near-by tree line we could see the **Philadelphia skyscrapers.**

Soon the trail enters a mixed forest and intersects with Ravine Loop. We headed downhill on an old, grassy road, passing a large grove of locust, oak, and maple trees on our left. The trail steepens as it heads

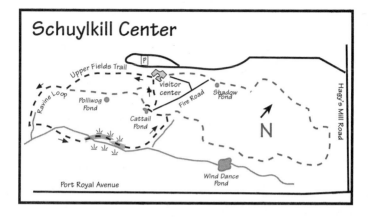

Schuylkill Center

Upper Fields Trail

P

Ravine Loop

visitor center

Polliwog Pond

Fire Road

Shadow Pond

Cattail Pond

N

Hagy's Mill Road

Wind Dance Pond

Port Royal Avenue

downhill. We crossed a footbridge and stream at the bottom, following the stream past a rocky outcrop to a second footbridge, where we crossed the stream again and ascended a steep hill along a fern-lined path—still deep in the woods. At this point, we noticed shiny quartz flecks all along the trail and quartz shining on the rocks alongside.

The vegetation that grows on steep hillsides varies depending on the quality, depth, compass orientation, and moisture content of the soil. Barren spots indicate thin and/or dry soils. Unseen seeps and springs, however, can provide moisture in unlikely places. Patches of lush green plant life give these wet areas away. Dense stands of moisture-loving ferns often cover the ground in these areas, and maples and locusts form a canopy that retards evaporation. Black locust grows quickly and spreads by sprouts. Its spreading root system helps hold the soil in place on steep banks. That's why it is often planted on reclaimed strip mines to prevent erosion.

Down at stream level again we crossed our third footbridge and passed between two large tulip poplar trees. We came to a wetlands area, which we crossed on a long, wooden boardwalk. We surprised two does and a fawn feeding near the water. We also observed frogs, wood duck boxes, and water skimmers.

Just past the wetlands, we entered a mature forest of large oaks and hickories. Climbing back toward the visitor center, the trail passes the ruins of an old springhouse. Up a short flight of stairs, it continues to Cattail Pond. The pond features a viewing platform but no cattails. From here, guides Nora and Emma took us on the Cattail Pond Trail to the Towhee Trail, which leads back to the visitor center.

Though Cattail Pond is small, it attracts marsh birds such as red-winged blackbirds and common yellowthroats. Watch for the brightly colored males of both species singing from the tops of the cattails' spike-like flower. Look closer at the cattail flower, and you'll see that it consists of two parts. Tiny, yellow male flowers grow above the more familiar cylinder of brown female flowers on each stem.

Don't miss the outstanding nature-oriented gift shop and the Discovery Room. The Discovery Room features many different interactive displays, such as the predator/prey matches, a giant magnifying lens, a dinosaur tar pit puppet show, puzzles, an aquarium with a corn snake, a giant "mole hole" to climb through, a rain forest pantry, pond succession, an observation beehive, a sandbox for making animal tracks, and much more. The Discovery Room alone is worth the trip to the Schuylkill Center.

A fritillary nectars on a thistle blossom.

Getting There

From the Schuylkill Expressway, take Exit 7A and proceed about 4.5 miles to Port Royal Avenue. Turn right (there's a sign for the center) and drive about 0.2 mile and turn right again (second right from Port Royal Avenue) onto Hagy's Mill Road. Drive 0.3 mile and turn left at entrance sign.

Facilities: Rest rooms and water fountains are available in the visitor center. There are also classrooms, a laboratory, a teacher resource center, and a computer learning center.

Best Time to Visit: This facility hosts many school groups, so we would suggest a weekend visit during the school year. Visit any time during the summer.

Special Note: All visitors must register at the nature center. Nature center and bookstore admission are free; trail admission is $5 for adults and $3 for children.

For More Information: Call the center at 215-482-7300.

Nearby Attractions: Philadelphia Zoo.

Cardinals—Everyone's Favorite Bird

It's a sight you'll never forget: a flock of bright red male cardinals perched in a drab, leafless tree on a snowy winter day. Their very presence brightens the day and lifts the spirit.

In the spring the male's song tells us warmer days lie just ahead. "What cheer! What cheer! What cheer!" or "Purdy, purdy, purdy," are just two of the familiar songs that let us identify cardinals by sound.

In the summer, after raising a brood or two, parent cardinals escort their family to backyard feeding stations. The elders introduce the young to their favorite fast food—sunflower seeds.

Finally, in the fall, family groups come together to form the flocks that later in the year will visit feeding stations. The colder and snowier the weather, the larger the flocks of cardinals seem to be.

Of all the birds that visit backyard feeders, none is more familiar or more welcome than the cardinal. The crested crimson male is certainly one of the most widely recognized and admired birds in America. In fact, seven states have honored the cardinal by naming it the state bird.

The male's brilliant red plumage and loud slurred whistles attract both attention and admiration from bird-watchers. But don't assume every singing cardinal is a male. Unlike most songbirds, female cardinals sing, too.

Cardinals are easy to recognize because they are our only red-crested bird. The reddish brown female pales in comparison to the brilliant scarlet male. Adults of both sexes have bright pink or red bills and black faces. Juveniles resemble adults but have dark bills.

Cardinal bills are massive and powerful. If ever a bird was meant to crack open and eat seeds, it's the cardinal. No wonder it is such a connoisseur of sunflower seeds.

Cardinals avoid deep forests and seem well adapted to habitat disturbances. Forest edges, old fields, parks, cemeteries, and fencerows attract them throughout the year.

A better understanding of cardinal behavior comes from carefully observing what occurs at backyard bird feeders. Though the pair bond relaxes, mated cardinals remain together in small loose flocks during the winter. During intense cold snaps, flocks of ten to twenty birds sometime gather. During January cold snaps, I sometimes count more than fifty in my backyard at one time.

Throughout the winter, males often eat their fill before allowing females access to the feeder. This behavior changes abruptly during spring courting, however. Then males not only permit females access to the feeder, they even husk the seeds and pass them, bill to bill, to the female. These "kisses" continue throughout the breeding season, serving to strengthen and maintain the bond.

One of the most interesting and commonly observed examples of cardinal behavior is their sometimes "crazed" attacks on windows. Usually in the spring (but I've had reports of this behavior at all times of year), seemingly suicidal cardinals repeatedly crash into large windows or glass patio doors. Occasionally casualties occur. Particularly aggressive cardinals can stun themselves or break their necks and die. If you find a stunned bird, put it in a paper bag, clip the bag securely, and place it in a dark area for an hour. Then release the bird. Stunned birds usually recover quickly.

Why do cardinals abuse themselves so? Male cardinals are strongly territorial, even during the nonbreeding season. Although their aggressive tendencies subside during fall and winter, territorial outbursts can occur at any time.

When a male cardinal sees his reflection in a window or even a hubcap, he responds as if there is a real rival. Sometimes his attacks last for an hour or more until more powerful urges—fatigue or hunger—prevail.

Despite these occasional bouts of "insanity," cardinals retain their favorite-bird status. At feeders, windows, or just passing through the yard, cardinals invariably monopolize the spotlight.

Bucks County

3. Bowman's Hill Wildflower Preserve
New Hope

Hours: Grounds, daily 8:00 A.M. to sunset. Headquarters, 9:00 A.M. to 5:00 P.M. Monday through Saturday, 12:00 to 5:00 P.M. on Sunday. Closed New Year's Day, Easter, Thanksgiving, and Christmas.

A wildflower wonderland awaits visitors to Bowman's Hill Wildflower Preserve. Twenty-six easy, well-maintained trails wind through the 80-acre preserve, but we had trouble actually walking because we were too busy enjoying the blooming wildflowers and trying to figure out those that were past bloom. This was one of Scott's favorite sites. As a wildflower and natural gardening enthusiast himself, he felt compelled to study closely those plants he didn't already know and note which attracted butterflies and other wildlife. And later, he really went wild at the sales shop, where we discovered a native wildflower sale in progress. We left that day with several 5-foot-tall joe-pye weed plants perched precariously in the back of our van.

Established in 1934, the preserve functions to protect Pennsylvania's native trees, flowers, shrubs, ferns, and

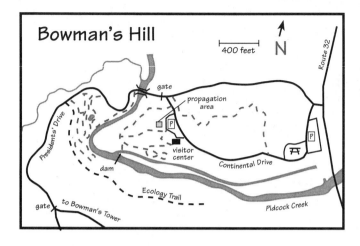

vines. The plants grow in natural settings in woodlands and meadows and along the banks of Pidcock Creek. Trails are well marked, and there are benches throughout. Be sure to pick up a trail map. The maps are well designed, detailed, and easy to follow. There are two different maps, one for spring and one for fall, and each includes an extensive listing of plant species by common name, scientific name, habitat, which trail they are found along, the exact distance along the trail at which you will find them, and in which month. There are even sketches of some of the more common wildflowers. It's impossible not to **learn a lot about wildflowers** and plants in this preserve.

We visited on a hazy August morning, and 5 minutes down the first trail we realized how smart we had been to use the insect repellent. Vegetation and water combine to make perfect habitat for many biting insects.

We explored most of the trails, which are short and intersecting. Along many, we noticed rare or endangered plants encased in plastic mesh. And encircling the entire preserve was a 10-foot-high chain-link fence. Both measures, we later confirmed, were efforts to protect the preserve from the ravages of deer browsing. There's even an automatic gate in the fence that allows visitors to enter and exit in their vehicles. The resident deer were driven out in winter of 1993, but by a year and a half later, some were back.

Among the most prolific wildflowers we saw that day were bright red, shade- and moisture-loving cardinal flowers; jack-in-the-pulpit, whose dull erect flower (jack) is surrounded and covered by a striped leaf-like spathe (the pulpit); bee balm, a bright red mint often visited by hummingbirds; New England aster; swamp rose mallow, a hibiscus whose long, fused stamens emerge as a pollen-laden column from the center of the flower; pungently aromatic skunk cabbage; and a variety of verdant ferns.

A paved road open only to pedestrians passes through the preserve. Along this road we found a large stand of eastern prickly pear cactus in full bloom. The paved road extends all the way to Bowman's Tower, a distance of 1 mile from the preserve headquarters. The 110-foot observation tower is located on the same site used by revolutionary soldiers to observe the Delaware River and a 14-mile stretch of the surrounding countryside. Built in 1930, the tower commemorates this lookout site. Visitors can take an elevator to the top. There's a modest admission charge, which goes to the preserve, and hours vary.

*A sea of brown-eyed Susans decorates a
Pennsylvania meadow.*

Guided tours of the preserve are available at 2:00
P.M. daily, for a small fee.

In addition to its trails and extensive plant collection, the preserve features special programs, events, and
exhibits. In the headquarters, wildflower watercolors

hang on the walls, and large windows allow visitors to watch birds at feeders outside. There is also a bird, egg, and nest collection. The gift shop sells wildflower seeds and plants, pressed flowers, and other nature items.

For more information, call the Washington Crossing Historic Park office (which administers the preserve) at 215-862-2924.

Getting There

Located along Rte. 32, 2.5 miles south of New Hope in the northern section of Washington Crossing Historic Park and 5.5 miles north of the park office in the southern section of the park. A large sign along the highway identifies the preserve entrance.

Nearby Attractions: Washington Crossing Historic Park, which encompasses the wildflower preserve, offers a fascinating look at Revolution-era life and an interpretation of that fateful Christmas night in 1776, when George Washington and his troops crossed the Delaware River and marched into Trenton to defeat the Hessians. There are two separate sections to the park property. The north section, which includes the preserve, features the Colonial-style house and outbuildings, a gristmill, Bowman's Tower, and soldiers' graves. The southern section contains the visitor center and various Colonial houses and inns used by the Continental army.

Historic New Hope, a village just 2.5 miles north of the preserve on Rte. 32, features art galleries, antique shops, craft shops, and various dining and entertainment opportunities.

4. Ralph Stover State Park
Pipersville

Hours: Daily, sunrise to sunset

Sheer rocky cliffs and turbulent white water attract and challenge the many visitors to Ralph Stover State Park. But the biggest challenge for us was just finding the park. We never would have if Linda's sister, who lives less than 2 miles away, hadn't personally escorted us. Navigating these tangled country roads is experiencing a little of what travel in the 1700s must have been like.

While the park draws large numbers of experienced rock climbers and serious kayakers, many others, like ourselves, come to enjoy the many easy walking trails and scenic vistas.

The 45-acre park consists of two separate parcels along Tohickon Creek. The larger parcel, location of the park headquarters, was once the site of an eighteenth-century water-powered grain mill. The second area is known as High Rocks. This area, donated by author and former Bucks County resident James A. Michener, overlooks a horseshoe bend in Tohickon Creek. It features sheer rocky cliffs and spectacular views. Many local hikers come to watch the rock climbers scaling a 200-foot cliff.

On a 57-degree day in December, we hiked a portion of the High Rocks Trail. The 0.75-mile trail connects the two sections of the park by way of Tohickon Valley Park,

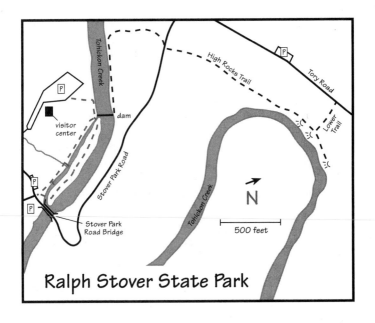

Ralph Stover State Park

a Bucks County park that lies between the two. We began hiking from a parking lot on the edge of the High Rocks section.

Winter hikes are great in areas featuring spectacular vistas. With the leaves gone, hikers have an unobstructed view. And indeed, on that sunny, warm day, Tohickon Creek sparkled and shimmered as it snaked far below us. The downside, of course, is the mud. Winter thaws leave most trails in soggy condition. Our older daughter slipped and fell in the mud before we were 100 yards from the car. Despite the allure of warm temperatures, we much prefer winter hikes when the ground is frozen.

High Rocks Trail at this point consists of two separate trails: High Trail and Lower Trail. High Trail follows the ridge top and offers easy, flat surfaces. We encountered several mountain bikers on this trail. The Lower Trail follows the cliff's edge just behind a high chain-link fence. This trail affords the best views, and the kids found it much more challenging and fun. Rocky and a little steep in some places, this trail gave them the thrill of rock climbing without us worrying about them falling over the cliff. This trail is not for older folks or little ones, but our five-year-old did well under our supervision.

Less than half a mile from the parking lot, the Lower Trail forks. The lower fork descends to the creek and becomes a more rugged, rock-climbing experience we recommend for hardier older children and adults. Fishermen take this trail to the creek. Hikers take it for the thrill of the descent and for a lovely walk along the creek to Tohickon Valley Park some 2.5 miles downstream. The upper fork joins the High Rocks Trail. With the children, this is the fork we took. We circled back to the parking lot via the High Rocks Trail.

Though rocks left behind by long-gone glaciers dominate this park, don't ignore the lush forest that characterizes the area. Take time, for example, to distinguish between **white oaks**, which have light-gray bark and smooth-edged lobed leaves, and **red oaks**, which have dark deeply furrowed bark and leaves whose lobes are distinctly toothed. Elsewhere, shagbark hickories live up to their name. Long shaggy strips of bark encircle the trunk, and each piece curves outward at its lower end. The presence of oaks and hickories lets you know you've entered a remnant of the once-vast eastern deciduous forest.

Abandoned stone fences are common in Pennsylvania woodlands.

To hike to the High Rocks area from the park headquarters, walk southeast a short way along Tohickon
Creek, cross the Stover Park Road bridge (closed to vehicles), proceed about 0.5 mile up the paved Stover Park

Road, then turn right onto the High Rocks Trail. At this point, it's another thousand feet or so to state parkland and the point at which we entered the trail with our children. If the trail is particularly muddy, you could proceed all the way up Stover Park Road to Tory Road, then turn right and follow Tory Road to the parking lot and trail access. To stay off paved roads completely, you could access the trail by crossing the dam at the headquarters and head east along the creek's north bank. But be forewarned: this steep and rough section south of Stover Park Road is no longer maintained. Park employees do not recommend this route, even though it is included on the map.

Secure a map at the headquarters before you hike, but be aware that it may not be completely accurate. For example, the one we picked up in December 1994 didn't indicate that the Stover Park Road bridge was closed, and it didn't differentiate between the High Trail and Lower Trail in the High Rocks section of the park.

In addition to hiking and rock climbing, park visitors can fish or whitewater canoe/kayak in Tohickon Creek. Also, six family cabins are rented to visitors from mid-April to late December. Camping is available at the adjacent Tohickon Valley Park. (Call Bucks County Parks for information at 215-757-0571.)

Getting There

Pay attention, because this is complicated. **To reach the park headquarters,** from Rte. 611 about 7 miles north of Doylestown turn east onto Rte. 413 at Pipersville and proceed 0.2 mile to a stop sign. Turn left (still on Rte. 413) and proceed another 0.2 mile to an intersection at the

Pipersville Inn. Go straight through the intersection (now on Dark Hollow Road) and travel 1.2 miles to Schlenk Road. Turn right (there's a sign for Stover Myers Mill Parking on the corner) and proceed 0.8 mile to Covered Bridge Road, passing through the covered bridge itself on the way. Turn left onto Covered Bridge Road and travel 0.6 mile to a stop sign. Turn left onto SR 1011 (there's no road sign, but this is Stump Road) and drive 0.8 mile, then turn left onto Park Office Road.

To reach High Rocks, proceed the same as above, except travel 2.3 miles past the intersection at Pipersville Inn to Stover Park Road. (The road is hidden, but there's a small sign on the left.) Turn right onto Stover Park Road and travel 0.8 mile to Tory Road. Turn left and proceed 0.2 mile to the parking area on the left. (There is a public telephone in the parking lot.) If you traveled another 0.5 mile on Stover Park Road beyond the Tory Road intersection, you would reach a bridge (now closed to vehicular traffic) that crosses the Tohickon Creek just east of park headquarters. This is the most direct link between the two parts of the park.

Nearby Attractions: Look for the old stone walls and Colonial-era houses all along the drive to the park office. One historical attraction, Stover Myers Mill, can be found right along Dark Hollow Road, just past the turnoff for the park headquarters.

5. Delaware Canal State Park

Easton–Bristol

Hours: Daily, 8:00 A.M. to sunset

During the nineteenth century, the Delaware Canal played a major role in the industrial revolution along the eastern seaboard. Mules walking along canalside paths towed about 33 million tons of anthracite coal destined for Philadelphia, New York, and other industrial centers. Another 6 million tons of food and miscellaneous cargo were hauled to communities along the 60-mile canal, from Easton to Bristol. Today those towpaths invite walkers and bicyclists to enjoy some of the prettiest scenery in Pennsylvania.

The towpath is a **National Heritage Trail**. Like the canal itself, it parallels the Delaware River. Except for about a 10-mile section below Yardley, southernmost portion, the trail is accessible its entire length. Hikers and bikers can access the trail at many different points. But unless you leave a second vehicle somewhere or make arrangements to be picked up, you must walk back to your original starting point. It's easy to get so caught up in sight-seeing and bird-watching that you forget how far you've gone and must face a return trip just as far.

One of the best access points we found was Virginia Forrest Recreation Area 3.5 miles north of Rte. 202 and New Hope. There are two parking areas just off Rte. 32, where picnic tables, benches, and rest rooms are located. The tow-

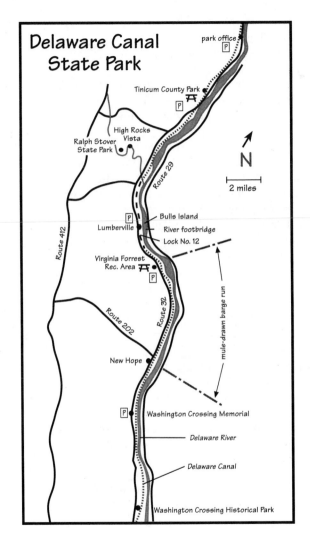

Delaware Canal State Park

park office 🅿

Tinicum County Park 🅿

High Rocks Vista
Ralph Stover State Park

Route 29

N
2 miles

🅿 Bulls Island
Lumberville ● River footbridge
Lock No. 12

Virginia Forrest Rec. Area
🅿

Route 412

Route 32

Route 202

mule-drawn barge run

New Hope ●

🅿 Washington Crossing Memorial

Delaware River

Delaware Canal

Washington Crossing Historical Park

path at this point is right beside the Delaware River. You can head either north or south from the parking area. We discovered a great 5-mile round-trip hike from this point.

We headed north, birding our way along this great riparian habitat. Several belted kingfishers, including one with a small fish in its bill, flew by overhead. Closer to ground level, we saw a white-eyed vireo, several hummingbirds, a great-crested flycatcher, a rose-breasted grosbeak, and several cardinals. From deep in the woods we heard the flutelike yodel of a wood thrush and just a few hoots from an apparently wide awake great horned owl. One mile north of the recreation area we passed through a small quarry area. And just 0.3 mile farther we came to the village of Lumberville. For about a mile, the towpath passes right behind the houses and businesses of this quaint little town. We found it fascinating, even if we did feel a bit like voyeurs.

Two and a half miles north of the recreation area and right in Lumberville we came to a footbridge across the Delaware River. We crossed the bridge, pacing off about 240 yards, and made a fascinating discovery: Bull's Island in the D&R Canal State Park of New Jersey. As a park ranger explained to us, the D&R Canal, part of an extensive canal system during the last century, now supplies drinking water for millions in New Jersey. Visitors canoe the canal and walk or ride bicycles along the towpath. Look for the cliff swallows nesting under the footbridge. We saw dozens, probably hundreds of their globular mud nests.

There are restaurants in Lumberville, and if you've packed a lunch, you can eat it on either side of the river. We opted for the New Jersey side. There were also portable toilets there and a park office with brochures

A Carolina chickadee prepares to leave its nesting cavity—in this case a nest box.

and information. We were well rested by the time we headed back to the Virginia Forrest Recreation Area and our waiting car.

If you want to explore the footbridge across the river without taking a long hike to get there, try parking at Lumberville Lock No. 12. There's a small parking area and several picnic tables.

Another good access point is at Tinicum County Park, about 8 miles north of Lumberville. Park beside the towpath and hike in either direction. The park features campsites, a playground, pit toilets, a Frisbee golf course, picnic tables, and a public boat access to the Delaware River just across the street (Rte. 32) from the park. From this point you can hike 3 miles north to the state park office.

Washington Crossing State Park and the town of New Hope are two other popular access points. Farther north, there are several parking areas/access spots just south of the Rtes. 32 and 611 intersection (near Narrowsville).

There are many other good access points—too many to describe here. We'd suggest stopping by the Delaware Canal State Park office just south of Upper Black Eddy to pick up a park brochure and map. Another strategy for those who have the time is just to take a leisurely drive along Rte. 32 (River Road) between Washington Crossing Historical Park and Narrowsville. Look for sections of the towpath that appeal to you. In the process, you can enjoy the Colonial-era houses and scenery of historic Bucks County.

When you get tired of walking, try a mule-drawn barge ride. There's a barge concession in New Hope, the arts and crafts tourist town located just about halfway along the 60-mile canal route.

History buffs will be interested to know that the canal is a National Historic Landmark. Almost perfectly intact except for the last 0.7 mile, the canal still has its locks, miter gates, aqueducts, and other operational and engineering features.

Getting There

The state park office is located in Lodi, just over 2 miles south of Upper Black Eddy along Rte. 32. A large roadside sign marks the entrance. The office is next to some maintenance sheds, and it's a little difficult to see at first.

For More Information: Call the park office at 610-982-5560.

6. Peace Valley Park
Doylestown

Hours: Dawn to dusk

Peace Valley Park is a popular recreational facility featuring the 365-acre Lake Galena. Boaters, fishermen, joggers, bikers, roller bladers, and others flock to its paved paths, docks, and picnic areas at the congested west end. Thousands of Canada geese also frequent this area, their droppings littering every path and open area. For nature hikers, we suggest the park's more secluded and "wild" east end. This area consists of a protected waterfowl area (about 0.3 of the lake's upper end), a nature center, and 9 miles of interconnected hiking trails through wetlands, uplands, fields, and forests. Trail combinations are endless, so you can take a serious hike or a light stroll—all on easy trail surfaces. The Pooh Tree Loop is graveled, but other trails are muddy at times. We recommend boots, especially if you hike during a winter thaw.

For a wonderful introduction to the area, **visit the nature center** before you hike. It features wildlife exhibits, bird feeding stations, hands-on exhibits, and a great gift shop. Ask for a trail map from the gift shop cashier, check for interesting bird sightings on the day you visit (posted in the nature center), then proceed on your walk. There are several short trails behind (west of) the nature center, on the lake's north shore. Most occur east of the nature center near the lake's three feeder

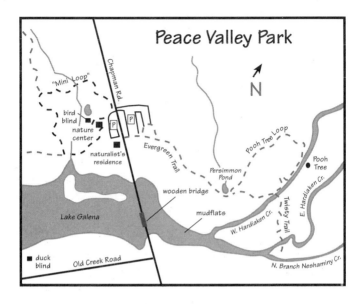

Peace Valley Park

"Mini Loop"

Chapman Rd.

bird blind

nature center

naturalist's residence

Evergreen Trail

Pooh Tree Loop

Persimmon Pond

Pooh Tree

E. Hardiaken Cr.

Twisty Trail

wooden bridge

mudflats

W. Hardiaken Cr.

Lake Galena

duck blind

Old Creek Road

N. Branch Neshaminy Cr.

N

streams: West Hardiaken Creek, East Hardiaken Creek, and North Branch of Neshaminy Creek. You can access these trails from the parking lot. Or you can take the more scenic route, as we did, and head south across a bridge. From the bridge, hikers can face west to view waterfowl on the lake or east to the mudflats and various shorebirds probing the mud for food. More than 250 species of birds have been sighted along the nature trails, many right in this refuge area. **Egrets and great blue herons** are common here, and even foraging **bald eagles** have been sighted. Spring, summer, and fall are the best times to view waterfowl. Recently, wild turkeys have taken up residence in the area of the nature trails, and confirmed bobcat sightings have been reported.

Proceeding across the bridge, we headed for the farthest hiking trail—the Morning Bird Walk. The entire way from the nature center to the Morning Bird trailhead is paved and is wheelchair accessible. But be aware that the road climbs a fair-sized hill past the bridge.

Morning Bird Walk follows the edge of a cornfield. Nest boxes parallel the trail here, and during the nesting season hikers can expect to see bluebirds, chickadees, titmice, and wrens. At its northern end, Morning Bird Walk intersects with Upper Woods Trail. You can continue north along the Upper Woods Trail and work your way around the perimeter of the entire area, or turn south, as we did, and wander along the maze of trails in the middle.

As the entire east end is only 360 acres, both east and west of the nature center, this is a wonderful area for allowing the older children to orienteer on their own. The trail map is easy to follow, the trails themselves are well marked, and children feel a wonderful sense of adventure and accomplishment when they can figure out how to get where they want to go.

Following our two daughters and their cousin Matthew, we snaked our way south along a wooded ridge until we came to the steep wooden steps leading to the North Branch of Neshaminy Creek below. We crossed the creek on a "boulder bridge" that the kids just loved. A few steps farther on, we crossed East Hardiaken Creek, this time on a small wooden bridge. We picked up Twisty Trail on the opposite bank and proceeded several hundred yards to West Hardiaken Creek, where we again crossed the water on rocks, much to the kids' delight. These three creeks are the feeder streams for

Lake Galena. The trails in these low-lying areas can get quite muddy.

Our third creek crossing landed us on the Pooh Tree Loop. The highlight of this centrally located loop trail, and the entire visit to Peace Valley, as far as five-year-old Emma was concerned, was the Pooh Tree. The hollowed-out base of this giant sycamore tree looks as if it could easily house that lovable Pooh Bear—and several kids, besides. We had trouble coaxing Emma out of the tree.

The entire Pooh Trail Loop is graveled. It is easily accessible from the parking lot via the Evergreen Trail. This would make an easy, clean, and enjoyable outing for less able hikers or very young children.

After traveling the loop counterclockwise and investigating the tiny Persimmon Pond at its southern tip—where we saw bullfrogs, green frogs, red-winged blackbirds, and a single common yellowthroat—we took the Evergreen Trail back to the parking lot. The children loved the pine needles blanketing the forest floor and couldn't resist lying down under a big conifer just to see how soft the needles really felt.

Our entire hike that warm winter day took just about an hour, including all of our stops to marvel at natural wonders. We're all anxious to return to explore the trails we didn't take.

Nature center trails are open daily from dawn until dusk. During snowy weather, some trails are open for cross-country skiing. The nature center itself is open from 9:00 A.M. to 5:00 P.M. every day but Monday. The nature center offers regularly scheduled guided family nature walks, weekly adult nature walks, full-moon hikes, and star watches. Call the center at 215-345-7860 for more information.

Getting There

From Rte. 313 2.5 miles west of Rte. 611 in Doylestown, turn south onto New Galena Road (at the sign for the Peace Valley Winery). Drive 0.7 mile, then turn left onto Chapman Road. Drive 0.5 mile to the nature center and nature center trails.

Nearby Attractions: Make time to explore other parts of the 1,500-acre Peace Valley Park. Your experiences elsewhere will probably not be as "wild" as in the nature center area, but you will certainly have close encounters with Canada geese. There are hiking and biking trails all along the lake, horseback riding trails, a fishing pier, boat docks, and other recreational facilities. For information, call the park office at 215-822-8608.

In nearby Doylestown, the Mercer Museum offers visitors an eclectic collection of antique artifacts that helped early Americans build a nation. More than fifty thousand items predating the Industrial Revolution are presented in a seven-story concrete structure complete with gables, towers, and parapets. There's also a nice collection of ancient Native American artifacts. We found it one of the most visually stimulating experiences we've ever had. It's like discovering a huge attic crammed with fascinating items. We highly recommend a visit. For information, call 215-345-0210.

7. Silver Lake Nature Center
Bristol

Hours: Grounds open sunrise to sunset daily

The Silver Lake Nature Center, another in a series of excellent Bucks County parks, carves out a wild niche right in the thick of Philadelphia suburbia. This 235-acre sanctuary lies in a geological area known as the Coastal Plain. As a **distinct geological area**, it features distinctive flora and fauna. There is also a lake on the center's eastern edge.

The area has an interesting history. In the early 1700s, colonists needed a power source for a mill on what's now Mill Street, so they dammed Otter Creek and created Silver Lake. In the later part of that century, the area of Bristol became famous for its baths, built along Bath Road. Visitors from all over came to bathe in the "healthful" tidal waters. Then, for about a century, the Mill Pond was largely ignored. During the Depression, it was dredged and used as a swimming spot. Today it's **home to countless ducks and geese** and is a popular picnic and hiking spot.

There are 3 miles of hiking trails within the park. Obtaining a trail map at the nature center, we set off one humid summer morning from the trailhead behind the center, heading east toward Otter Creek. Within minutes we saw squirrels, chipmunks, a rabbit, and a flock of robins.

The dirt path bears left across a small footbridge, then right across a narrow boardwalk. The bird life was active in the vicinity of that boardwalk, and we soon saw chickadees, blue jays, downy woodpeckers, grackles, cardinals, and a flicker. The trail brochure claims that more than 160 species can be found on the park grounds.

The boardwalk passes through a boggy area of water lilies, mallows, and flowering purple loosestrife. It continues to another boardwalk and viewing platform overlooking the creek. In mid-August, we found an

Buttonbush at Silver Lake.

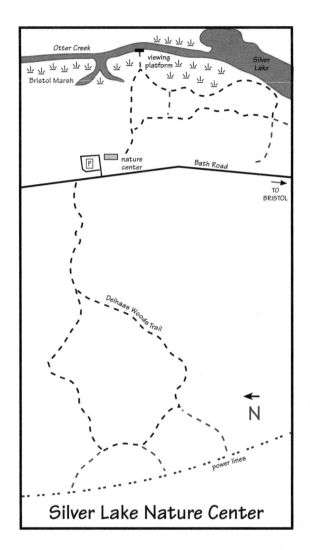

Otter Creek

Bristol Marsh

viewing platform

Silver Lake

nature center

Bath Road

P

TO BRISTOL

Delhaas Woods Trail

N

power lines

Silver Lake Nature Center

abundance of flowering purple loosestrife and big white and pink mallows. Sedges and buttonbush were also prominent. A family of mallards lazily paddled by. This whole tidal area is known as Bristol Marsh, and the nature center offers many different programs exploring this fascinating and rich ecosystem.

Past the overlook, the trail turns right (south) and skirts the water's edge. We could see from the map that we were heading toward Silver Lake. There are some large maples, elms, and oaks along the well-maintained trail.

The trail emerges on the edge of the lake. At water's edge we encountered a mallard hen and two large ducklings. Just a few yards away was another hen and her brood hiding in the high grass. Soon we could see that the lake was inundated with mallards, Canada geese, and an array of hybrids. (Personally, we feel the lake could be improved with a little waterfowl management and population control: waterfowl feathers and droppings litter the trail.)

The trail soon cuts back north into the woods again and back to the nature center. The whole loop took us less than an hour, and we traveled at a very leisurely pace, stopping frequently to observe plants and wildlife. The entire time we hiked we encountered only one jogger, one bicyclist, and two elderly men feeding ducks.

A short spur connects the two parallel legs of the loop, so you could take an even shorter hike, basically circling out to the marshy area and back. There is also a trail north of the nature center, accessible from either the parking lot or the trail leading out to the creek. This trail loops through a wooded area and back.

But the bulk of the Silver Lake Nature Center trail system lies west of the center, on the opposite side of Bath Road. This area of interconnecting paths is known as the Delhaas Woods Trail. The trailhead is just across the street from the nature center. Crossing this busy road is dangerous, so be careful!

The trail surface along the more than 2 miles of trail varies from packed dirt to stretches of gravel to several short boardwalks. The trail passes through woods, wetlands, and overgrown fields near a power line right-of-way. This is lowland floodplain area, so there are many boggy patches and millions of mosquitoes! Wear insect repellent! This is one hike we'd recommend taking in the heat of the day, when flying insects are not as active.

A great-crested flycatcher greeted us right at the boardwalk near the Delhaas Woods trailhead. From the trailhead, we walked into the woods on a boardwalk past a marshy area. Among the first things we noticed were lots of fungi at the beginning of the trail and sweet gum trees everywhere. Sweet gum, apparently named for the medicinal properties of its sap (its effects are "sweet"), is easily recognized by its large star-shaped leaves and its prickly spherical fruits, which measure about 1.5 inches in diameter. By mid-summer the fruits litter the trails. In the fall sweet gum leaves turn brilliant red and become one of the most spectacular trees in the woods.

There are several different forks in the trail and several ways to loop around the area (consult your trail map), but eventually the various forks all lead to an open power line right-of-way near the property's west edge.

Sweet gum has star-shaped leaves and thrives in wet areas.

As we hiked, we noticed an unusual amount of broken glass on the trail. There was a small amount of litter and other evidence of humans but not nearly as much as the glass. We suspect this reflects a shortage of staff and funding to maintain the trails.

We discovered that the power line right-of-way is a good birding spot, as open areas along wooded edges usually are. We saw and/or heard cardinals, towhees, indigo buntings, song sparrows, white-eyed vireos, a yellow warbler, chickadees, and field sparrows.

The Silver Lake Nature Center provides a great half-day of hiking and adventure. Make sure your visit includes a browse through the nature center building. There you'll see a freshwater aquarium; a terrarium; dioramas with mounted animals; dioramas with live animals; a man-made tree that demonstrates how an owl, flicker, raccoon, and bat can all live together; and more. Outside, on the north side of the building near the parking lot, is a butterfly garden. Late spring and summer are the best times to enjoy this interesting feature.

The nature center also offers numerous special programs, day camps, and natural explorations. Call for current information.

Getting There

From the Delaware Valley exit on the PA Turnpike (the last exit), take Rte. 13 south toward Bristol. At the second light turn right onto Bath Road. Drive 0.9 mile to the Silver Lake Nature Center and parking lot on the right.

Facilities: Excellent nature center and gift shop, open Tuesday through Saturday 10:00 A.M. to 5:00 P.M.; Sunday noon to 5:00 P.M. Closed Monday.

Best Time to Visit: Any time. The fall foliage would be spectacular, especially the brilliant red leaves of the sweet gum trees. During the summer, weekdays would be less crowded than weekends, especially around the lake.

Special Note: Much of the grounds include weedy or wooded wetlands, where mosquitoes thrive. Hats, long pants and sleeves, and insect repellent all will make your hike more enjoyable during the hot months. Insect repellent is especially recommended for the Delhaas Woods Trail west of the nature center and Bath Road.

For More Information: Call the nature center at 215-785-1177.

Nearby Attractions: Just a few miles south of Silver Lake and just east of I-95 on the Delaware River lies Neshaminy State Park. Though most visitors come to Neshaminy to launch boats on the Delaware River or to swim in the main pool, 4 miles of nature trails wander through the park. The River Walk Trail gives hikers a fascinating glimpse of big river ecology. Be sure to pick up a trail guide at the park office before starting. The most unusual aspect of the park is that even 116 miles from the ocean, tidal influences are noticeable. As high and low tides rise and fall, the river level can rise or fall an inch an hour. Despite this tidal influence, the river at this point is completely freshwater and just a remnant of the pristine riparian zone colonists found here 250 years ago.

Raccoons:
Ring-tailed Rascals

They arrive several hours after sunset. First, they raid the garden. So much for the sweet corn and ripe tomatoes. Next they attack the bird feeders and the garbage cans where we store the bird food. Then they terrorize the dog while emptying her dish. Finally, they climb onto the porch to wreak their havoc. It doesn't matter that's there is nothing edible on the porch; they just seem to enjoy tearing things up.

They are the night stalkers. Raccoons—the masked, ring-tailed rascals that originated search-and-destroy missions.

Occasional encounters with nocturnal wildlife are expected and even enjoyed by people who have chosen the country life. But when destructive visits occur every night, it gets old fast. Add a few misguided "animal lovers" who hand-feed raccoons on their back porch, and you've got a recipe for trouble.

I enjoy raccoons as much as anyone. But throughout much of the East, raccoons are out of control. I've counted as many as eight in the backyard at one time. A few years ago I live-trapped and removed ten. Nearby neighbors removed at least twenty-seven more. And still they come.

Raccoons are nothing if not adaptable. They live just about anywhere—in woods, fields, swamps, marshes, urban backyards, and abandoned buildings. They'll den in a hollow tree, an old groundhog burrow, a culvert, an unused chimney, a barn, or an attic. And they eat just about anything—acorns, apples, cherries, peaches, grapes, watermelons, corn, grasses, mushrooms, fish, crayfish, insects, earthworms, mice, moles, rabbits, chipmunks, birds and their eggs, carrion, and, of course, garbage. As long as there are people, raccoons will never go hungry.

Though adult raccoons are solitary, they are not territorial. So, though they don't go looking for company on their nightly forays, they usually don't fight if they meet another coon.

Adult females violate the solitary lifestyle for most of the summer and fall when they wander each night with their litter of three to five kits in tow. Only after plunging temperatures and snow announce the arrival of winter does she abandon the kits and hole up by herself. The young ones remain as a family unit and usually den together for the winter. On mild winter nights they leave their dens in search of mid-winter snacks.

By March, adult males wander in search of yearling and adult females. (Males don't breed until their second year.) In late May after a sixty-three-day gestation period, two to five kits are born. Development is slow; kits don't leave the den until they are eight to twelve weeks old. Then they begin following mom on her nightly foraging runs. Weaning occurs at sixteen weeks, but the pups remain with their mother until she leaves them in November or December.

In addition to abundant food and habitat, raccoons prosper because they have few natural predators. Mountain lions and wolves are distant memories in these parts. Only great horned owls, coyotes, and bobcats remain as potential predators, and they cover such large areas that they can't begin to control raccoon populations. That's left to automobiles, parasites, and diseases such as distemper and rabies. It took an outbreak of these two diseases in recent years to control an exploding raccoon population in eastern Maryland and Pennsylvania.

What about hunters and trappers, you ask? Good question. Coon hunting has limited appeal. It requires expensive, well-trained hounds, is physically exhausting, and is done at night. It's not exactly a growth sport in a couch-potato society.

The outlook for trapping is equally dismal. Fur prices have been down for years. Many trappers feel it's just not worth their time and effort.

That leaves us with a rapidly growing raccoon population that can take the joy out of country life. If you've got a coon problem, you're left with two choices. Handle it yourself. Or check the Yellow Pages under "Wildlife Damage Control."

One final bit of advice as you explore natural areas: *Never* pet, feed, or touch any wild mammal, especially raccoons. Only sick animals roam about during daylight hours and appear to be friendly. Don't be fooled. Raccoons, and all mammals for that matter, can carry rabies. Most human infections come when people approach a seemingly friendly animal. Interpret friendliness or fearlessness by wild animals as signs of illness and you will be safe. The one thing you should do is report suspicious animals to any staff member that might be handy.

8. Tyler State Park
Newtown

Hours: 8:00 A.M. to sunset daily

Neshaminy Creek meanders through the 1,711 acres of Tyler State Park. Originally part of a large farm and country estate, the park **retains its country charm**, featuring several original stone buildings dating back to the early 1700s. Visitors are free to hike anywhere along the 10.5 miles of bicycle trails, 9.0 miles of bridle trails, and 4.0 miles of hiking trails.

We'd suggest the Nature Trail in the center of the park. Drive to the end of the Main Park Road and park in the boat concession parking lot. The trail begins just on the other side of the pedestrian causeway across Neshaminy Creek (a popular fishing area).

Less than 0.5 mile in length, this small, dirt trail requires some rigorous hiking up through a ravine and back again, passing over rocks and exposed roots. Porter Run flows through the ravine to the creek, and the trail follows both sides of the run. Numerous trail spurs lead to the edge of the water.

Several hundred feet from the trailhead, a spur to the right leads up a steep, rocky hillside for about 200 yards to a grassy level area overlooking the valley and Neshaminy Creek below. It's a beautiful view, although the overlook area was weedy and overgrown when we visited in July. We simply waded through the weeds and

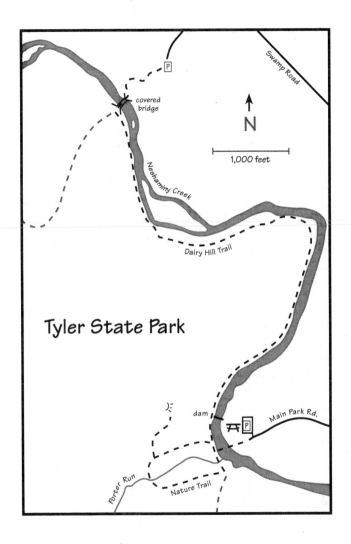

Tyler State Park

covered bridge

Neshaminy Creek

Dairy Hill Trail

Swamp Road

N

1,000 feet

dam

Main Park Rd.

Porter Run

Nature Trail

stepped up on a rail fence to get a better look. One-quarter of the park is leased to farmers, and we could see their farm fields on the other side of the creek. In the woods just before the grassy overlook area, huge oaks and beech trees tower above other woodland species. We observed robins, nuthatches, house wrens, chickadees, a wood thrush, and titmice here.

Back on the main trail, we continued up the ravine. The trail veers closer to the water at this point, and we could see the rocky escarpment on the opposite side. Just past a huge fallen tree, the trail forks. The fork was unmarked, so we bore left and continued to follow the run. Here, the trail passed several large boulders and a giant tulip poplar on the left. Tulip poplars grow straighter and taller than any tree in the eastern woods. Heights of 100 to 150 feet are common, and 200-foot specimens are known from the southern Appalachians.

Despite its name, this tree is not a true poplar. Named for its tulip-shaped leaves and blossoms, tulip trees, or yellow poplars as lumberjacks often call them, are classified as members of the magnolia family. Bees pollinate the large yellow-green flowers, and in some areas blood-red tulip honey is considered a delicacy.

Just past the poplar tree, the trail crosses a small, rocky ravine (seasonal run) and then passes over a few boulders and up over a huge fallen tree. (We admired the squarish rock slab pulled up by the roots when the tree toppled.) Here the trail forks again, and again we took the left fork and picked our way across the rock-strewn stream. After climbing the opposite bank (a steep and slippery challenge), we began to loop back down Porter Run ravine toward Neshaminy Creek.

View from a hilltop in Tyler State Park.

We passed a giant snag (standing dead tree) on the right at the top of the creek bank. Based on the number of old woodpecker holes and natural cavities in this aging skeleton, many birds and mammals have called this old tree home. The size of the excavated holes indicates that downy and pileated woodpeckers used the tree, and no doubt raccoons and opossums have occupied some of the larger natural cavities. Tree frogs, rat snakes, and myriad spiders and insects also find safe haven in abandoned cavities.

Soon we came to another fork. The left fork descends a steep, graveled hill down to the creek again. You could cross the creek and continue back on the original trail, or you could fork right and continue down on a hill high above the stream. This upper trail soon joins a wider, rough, and rocky trail, which we followed back to Neshaminy Creek.

This nature trail is supposed to be a self-guided trail with accompanying brochure, but apparently the park no longer maintains the trail markers or issues the interpretive brochure. Also, there didn't appear to be much of an effort to keep bicyclists out, even though a large sign clearly states that this area is off-limits to bicycles. (Actually, bicycles are restricted to the paved trails throughout the entire park.) We couldn't get an explanation why, but we think it's unfortunate. This a wonderful natural area with lots to see and learn. Perhaps this situation is evidence of the fact that state and national parks simply no longer have the resources to maintain facilities properly. None of us wants to pay taxes, but without public support our parks suffer—and so do we.

There are restrooms and a water fountain at the causeway picnic pavilion. We saw barn swallows nesting in the pavilion. They had lined their nests with goose and duck feathers.

Another good hiking area is at the park's north end, site of the Schofield Ford Covered Bridge. Built in 1874, the bridge was the longest covered bridge in Bucks County. Unfortunately, it burned in 1991. But at the time of our visit it was being restored with authentic materials and methods supplied by concerned local citizens. The bridge is accessible from the center of the park via various bike and equestrian trails (see park map), but we'd suggest driving to the park's north end and parking in the lot off Swamp Road (about 1.5 miles northwest of park office and Swamp Road entry).

From the parking lot, follow the dirt road (or hillside steps) down the hill to the bridge, about 0.25 mile. The covered bridge hiking/biking trail continues on the other side of the bridge. It interconnects with a streamside equestrian trail and several other trails, so you can customize a hike to suit your purposes.

Another interesting little walk involves following an old farm road through a field from the parking lot to a scenic overlook less than 0.5 mile away on a bank high above Neshaminy Creek. We saw countless butterflies and birds along this little spur, and we spent some time watching a kingfisher fishing for its meal in the creek below the overlook.

We found the covered bridge area to be a fascinating historical and biological site, and we were the only people there on the summer day we visited the park.

Getting There

From I-95, take Exit 30 onto Rte. 332 (Yardley/Newtown). Head west on Rte. 332 and drive 5 miles to the park entrance on the right. Or, from Exit 30, drive west on the 4-lane bypass around Newtown. The main park entrance is at the intersection of the bypass and Swamp Road.

Facilities: Picnic areas; ball fields; hiking, biking, and bridle trails; canoe concession; youth hostel; and facilities for the disabled.

Best Time to Visit: This park is heavily visited on summer weekends, so we would suggest a summer weekday visit. It's less crowded at other times of the year.

For More Information: Call the park office at 215-968-2021.

Nearby Attractions: Langhorne Players Theater and the Pennsylvania Guild of Craftsman Craft Center are both located in the southern part of the park. Bucks County Community College lies adjacent to the park's east end.

9. Nockamixon State Park
Quakertown

Hours: 8:00 A.M. to sunset, April 1 through October 31

Known primarily for its **large, undeveloped lake** and sailing opportunities, Nockamixon State Park also offers close, natural encounters for landlubbers in its Environmental Education Area. Located at the southwestern edge of the park, this area contains some 3.5 miles of interconnecting hiking trails. (Secure a detailed trail guide at the park office or marina visitor center.)

Access to the Environmental Education Area is just off Rte. 563, about 0.5 mile north of PA 313. From the parking lot, we headed toward the trailhead for three of the four marked trails in this area, alongside the remnants of an old stone fence. Here you have the choice of heading northeast (left) along the Community Loop, or heading southeast toward the lake and Tree Identification Trail, as we did. If you choose the Community Loop, you also have the option of turning left onto Woodland Walk, which eventually crosses Rte. 563 and leads to the Weisel Youth Hostel.

Past a short series of steps, the trail comes to a lily pad–covered pond. Here we stopped to listen to (and try to glimpse) **bullfrogs and green frogs**. This is one of the best places in the whole area, and you could spend a lot of time just observing here, as we did. We look for

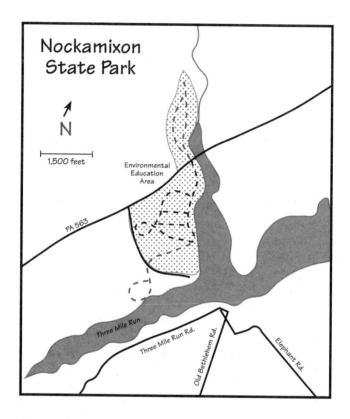

Nockamixon
State Park

↑
N

1,500 feet

Environmental
Education
Area

PA 563

Three Mile Run

Three Mile Run Rd.

Old Bethlehem Rd.

Elephant Rd.

frogs whenever we are near water. The presence or
absence of frogs generally indicates environmental
quality. Amphibian populations are rapidly declining
worldwide. Biologists consider it a crisis situation, and
they aren't sure exactly what's causing these populations to plummet. Most believe it is sensitivity to envi-

ronmental pollutants and water quality. This certainly makes sense because most amphibians lay their eggs in water. Other detrimental factors include habitat destruction and loss, drought, and over-harvesting of some species for food.

What first caught our attention that warm evening was a solitary bullfrog bellowing, "Jug-o-rum, jug-o-rum." The low, vibrating mating call seemed to emanate from the emergent vegetation just ahead, so we stopped and began scanning the shoreline with our binoculars. Sure enough, after several patient minutes, we spotted the handsome Romeo partially submerged at water's edge. Its back appeared greenish brown (well camouflaged amidst the murky water and pond vegetation) and from what we could see, it was probably about 5 inches long.

Bullfrogs are the largest frog species in North America. They can reach a length of 7 inches from snout to vent (hind end). During winter, they bury themselves in the muddy bottoms of ponds or rivers. They emerge from this hibernation in early March, and they begin the well-known mating calls in May. Typically, males such as the one we observed select a spot along the bank and call from the same location night after night. They rarely leave water's edge, where they can feed and mate and live a comfortable life.

We continued to watch the bullfrog, hoping to glimpse amplexus—a mating embrace. But what we actually saw was just as interesting. When a dragonfly ventured too near, the bullfrog simply zapped it with its long sticky tongue, and the insect disappeared. It happened so fast we had to confirm with each other that we had even seen it.

Bullfrogs are voracious predators. They'll eat anything they can swallow, including fish, birds, turtles, toads, rodents, snakes, and other frogs. There are even accounts of bullfrogs in Florida eating baby alligators.

Like other frogs, bullfrogs lay their eggs in large, gelatinous masses. We scanned the water and aquatic vegetation for the frothy-looking masses, but had no luck.

As we moved to continue our hike, we startled the bullfrog, and it leaped farther into the water, plopping loudly out of sight.

The trail continues as a short boardwalk across one end of the pond, then cuts back along the opposite shore, where we searched for frogs again. This time, we looked for the smaller green frog, which is easily identified by a call that sounds like a banjo string being plucked. Our movements must have startled some frogs, for we soon heard the telltale "plops" along water's edge. Again, persistence with the binoculars paid off, and it wasn't too long before we saw a green frog emerge near the shore. It faced us, and we could see the yellow throat that identified it as a male.

Green frogs can vary in color from a greenish brown to a gray. They can reach about 4 inches in length, with the females generally larger than the males. Like bullfrogs, green frogs spend most of their time in a favorite spot at water's edge, hunting for prey. They primarily eat insects and spiders. These solitary frogs make a call that sounds like a low-pitched "K-tong" and is repeated two or three times in a row.

An eastern kingbird is identified by its white terminal tail band.

The one we observed must have eaten recently or else sensed our presence, for it simply sat motionless for about 5 minutes. We gave up and continued the hike. Just beyond the pond, on a short spur to the right, is a building with toilets and a water fountain. A picnic pavilion is nearby. A wide, grassy swathe cut between the building and the pavilion serves as a trail. We followed it through a pine plantation, then soon turned left at a trail intersection and continued along Tree Identification Trail. (Turning right here would take you back to the second parking area and the trailhead for the Viburnum Loop.) Most of the trees in this densely wooded area are pines. A trail spur leads right to the water's edge. The trail parallels the lake's edge for awhile, through a multiflora rose thicket. The map shows it continuing, but we turned back at this point because the trail was overgrown and difficult to negotiate.

The trails loop and intersect the Environmental Educational Area, so it's possible to hike as long or as little as you want.

The park also features a 2.8-mile bicycle trail and 20 miles of equestrian trails.

Getting There

Nockamixon State Park lies 5.0 miles east of Quakertown and 9.0 miles west of Doylestown, just off Rte. 313. From Quakertown, travel east 5.0 miles on Rte. 313 from the junction of 663 and 309 (663 becomes 313). Turn left onto Rte. 563 and go 3.6 miles to the park entrance and main office. (The Environmental Education and trail area is before the park office, only about 0.5 mile after the turnoff onto Rte. 563.) From the northwest and Rte. 611, exit 611 on Rte. 412 and head north for 0.5 mile. Turn left (south) onto Rte. 563 and drive 4.3 miles to the park office. From the southwest, take Rte. 611 to Rte. 313, head west on 313 about 10 miles to Rte. 563. Turn right and proceed 3.6 miles to the park office.

Facilities: The Weisel Youth Hostel (215-536-8749) is located in the northwest corner of the park. The park also features a swimming pool with food concession, marina and boat rentals, more than five hundred picnic tables, comfort stations, and a large undeveloped lake. Nearby are private campgrounds and concessions renting horses.

Best Time to Visit: Any time.

For More Information: Call the park office at 215-529-7300.

Nearby Attractions: Lake Towhee County Park, 3 miles from the state park office, features facilities for hiking, fishing, camping, and picnicking. The 2,000-acre State Game Lands No. 157, just north of the park, offers a rifle range and areas for hiking and hunting. Also nearby is Peace Valley Park (see p. 33).

Montgomery County

10. Valley Forge National Historical Park
Valley Forge

Hours: Daily, 9:00 A.M. to 5:00 P.M.
Grounds sunrise to sunset.

Despite its reputation as one of southeastern Pennsylvania's major tourist destinations, Valley Forge National Historical Park has a lot to offer in the way of nature hikes. There are 12 miles of hiking/biking trails, including a 6-mile paved, multipurpose trail. Hikers can also wander among the miles and miles of fields and forests stretching across the park.

Our recommendation for the **most scenic, least frequented trail is the Valley Creek Trail.** Situated at the park's west end, the level, mostly paved trail extends for a mile along Valley Creek between Washington's Headquarters and Maxwell's Quarters. Unlike the other trails, this one is supposed to be just for hikers. (The bike and fitness crowd is more interested in the River Trail.) On a warm summer weekend, we encountered only two other walkers along this trail.

To access Valley Creek Trail from Washington's Headquarters, cross Rte. 23 and walk west, crossing the stone bridge. Turn left along the gravel road just past the

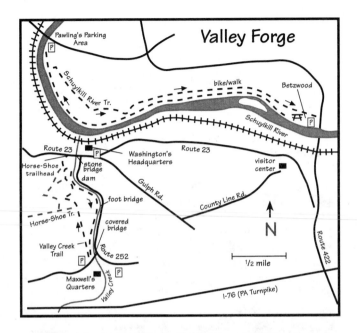

bridge (at the Sons of America sign) and follow the yellow blazes up a hill. Continue to follow the wide gravel trail. At the first major fork, bear left to the creek and the dam at the bottom of the hill.

This small dam is a lovely spot to sit and contemplate your surroundings, mesmerized by the sound of falling water. Pay attention for birds, too. There are many in this rich riparian zone. Continue along the creek for another mile, where the trail ends at a covered bridge and a small parking lot opposite Maxwell's Quarters. You can then backtrack to Washington's Headquarters, as we did, or have a ride waiting at the bridge. (There's also a small parking area at about midpoint along the trail, off Rte.

252, which parallels the creek on the opposite shore. Here you can access the trail via a small footbridge.)

The Schuylkill River Trail, by far the most popular trail, gently winds 3.0 miles along the river's wooded north shore from the Betzwood Picnic Area west to Pawling's Parking Area. A 2.3-mile loop trail is part of the river trail.

Popular with bicyclists, this wide trail easily accommodates hikers, too, and we enjoyed a leisurely stroll on a hot summer day. During the Revolutionary War, this area contained cattle herds, flatboats, and military supplies. Today there are huge maples and other hardwoods and lots of poison ivy ("Leaflets three, let it be.") growing trailside. Towering sycamores, identified by their flaking white bark, provide ample shade and many natural cavities for squirrels, raccoons, opossums, climbing snakes, and tree frogs. Trail markers note historical sites,

A bend in the Schuylkill River at Valley Forge.

Valley Forge visitor center.

and the occasional trailside bench provides rest for weary legs and feet. Short trail spurs lead down to the water's edge, and we observed many mallard ducks along the river. Two great blue herons fished the shallows off an island near the trailhead.

Also popular, especially with bicyclists, is a paved, 6-mile multipurpose trail.

For long-distance hikers and backpackers, the 130-mile Horse-Shoe Trail starts at Valley Forge Park and continues west, where it meets the Appalachian Trail north of Hershey. The trail ("Horse" for riders, "Shoe" for hikers) passes through Hopewell Furnace, French Creek State Park, Cornwall Furnace, Mt. Gretna, and the fields and forests of southeastern Pennsylvania. Some parts of the trail have been in use since the mid-eighteenth century, when the trail linked iron ore forges and furnaces along its route.

Getting There

From US Rte. 422, take Rte. 23 west and drive straight into the park at the visitor center. (The park entrance is just off Rte. 422.) To get to Valley Creek Trail from the park's main entrance, turn west at the stoplight and travel about 3 miles to Washington's Headquarters. You can park here, or turn left at the light onto Rte. 252 and park in a small lot opposite Maxwell's Quarters, a mile away at the other end of the trail. Also, there is a small parking lot and footbridge right along Rte. 252 in the middle of the trail. To get to the Schuylkill River Trail, from Rte. 422 west of the park, take Rte. 363 (Audubon/Trooper exit). Turn left at the stop sign and continue left down a steep hill to a large parking lot beside the river. This area is known as the Betzwood Picnic Area.

Facilities: A visitor center at the main entrance features a 15-minute film (played every 30 minutes) on the Valley Forge story. Exhibits include firearms and military accessories. Information on picnic areas, bicycle rentals, guided bus tours, and other park features, including special summer programs and demonstrations, is available at the visitor center.

Best Time to Visit: This park is a popular tourist destination, so crowds will be much larger during the summer months, particularly on the weekends. Even at other times of the year, many local residents use the park on weekends for bicycling and recreation. Your best bet is to visit during the week in spring, fall, or winter. Most trails are graveled or paved, so wet conditions are not much of a problem.

Nearby Attractions: Mill Grove, home of John James Audubon, is located several miles north of the park.

For More Information: Call park office at 610-783-1000.

11. Mill Grove (Audubon Wildlife Sanctuary)
Audubon

Hours: 7:00 A.M. to dusk; closed Mondays

Mill Grove, the **first American home of artist and naturalist John James Audubon,** is one of the Philadelphia area's best-kept secrets. There are no signs along nearby highways (or anywhere, except on the grounds themselves), and local people we've asked for directions looked at us blankly and claimed never to have heard of the place.

But Mill Grove is a place not to be missed by any nature lover. Four miles of gentle trails and the museum/homestead featuring much of the artist's work combine to offer an enjoyable, educational visit.

Mill Grove is more shrine than museum. Located high atop a hill overlooking the Perkiomen Creek in Montgomery County, the estate served as John James Audubon's home from 1804 to 1806. During this brief period in young Audubon's life, birds caught his fancy. Later he became the first wildlife artist to depict his subjects in natural settings.

Born in what is now Haiti in 1785, Audubon grew up in France and moved to America to supervise his father's estate at Mill Grove when he was just eighteen years old. Captivated by Mill Grove's abundant wildlife,

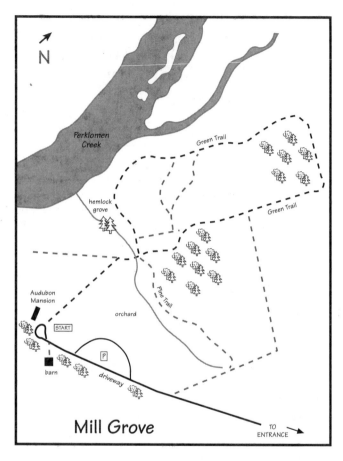

Mill Grove

young Audubon spent his first years in America hunting, trapping, watching birds, and sketching. He became a skilled outdoorsman, naturalist, and artist.

While at Mill Grove, Audubon discovered that limp, lifeless models (he shot many of his subjects) made painting lifelike images quite a challenge. "But alas! They were dead, to all intents and purposes, neither wing, leg nor tail could I place according to my wishes," he later wrote.

One morning Audubon awoke with an inspired solution to his problem, a solution that would characterize many of his future works. He dashed to nearby Norristown, bought some wire, and, upon his return, shot the first bird he saw—a kingfisher. He then skewered the bird's wings, legs, and body until "there stood before me the real kingfisher." This wire armature proved to be the tool that allowed Audubon to bring the victims of his gun back to life on canvas.

During Audubon's first year at Mill Grove, he made one of his greatest contributions to ornithology. He discovered a nest of phoebes in a rocky cave and attached "silver threads" to their legs. He hoped to see if the birds would ever return to Mill Grove. The next year, in spring 1805, he observed an adult phoebe with a silver thread on its leg tending a nest. Modern bird banding traces its roots to John James Audubon, a silver thread, and that phoebe.

Since 1951 Montgomery County has maintained Mill Grove as a museum and wildlife sanctuary for all to enjoy. In 1989 it was designated a National Historic Landmark.

The walls of the house are decorated with many of Audubon's classic works, including a recently restored, life-size original of a golden eagle taking a lamb. The other furnishings are early 1800s vintage, giving the house a historic appeal.

J. J. Audubon house at Mill Grove.

After touring the house, which takes about an hour, walk some of the easy trails snaking through the 175-acre estate (a trail map is available). The Green Trail, just less than 1 mile, proceeds from the mansion up a hill, then runs along a steep wooded slope overlooking the Perkiomen Creek. Most of the trail passes through woods. Even on a gray late December morning we counted a dozen species of birds. Return visits in spring and summer yielded close to fifty species, including a variety of warblers and vireos.

Don't miss the large trees gracing the grounds immediately surrounding the house. These trees are all labeled and are superb specimens (we couldn't resist hugging a few). An hour spent studying these labeled trees will go a long way toward helping anyone distinguish among the various oaks, maples, and other hardwoods that dominate the eastern deciduous forest.

Serious birders should inquire at the museum about an unmarked, grassy birding trail on 43 acres south of the mansion. This trail is not advertised, but you can request access.

Getting There

From Rte. 422 just north of Valley Forge National Historical Park, exit onto Rte. 363 and head north. Barely 0.1 mile from the exit, turn left at the first light onto Audubon Road. Drive 1.1 miles to a stop sign at a T. The Mill Grove entrance is directly across from the stop sign.

Facilities: The museum houses a small, but impressive, gift shop. Restrooms are available.

Nearby Attractions: Valley Forge National Historical Park, Evansburg State Park, the Philadelphia Zoo.

12. Green Lane Reservoir Park

Green Lane

Hours: Trails are open dawn to dusk

Hikers and nature lovers will find a lot to do at the Green Lane Reservoir Park. Although much of its 2,491 acres is covered by water, the surrounding woods and fields provide some of the **best birding and hiking** in the Philadelphia area. We will feature three main areas: the hiking trail at the main office and marina; the nature trail and butterfly garden at the nature center; and the water-fowl sanctuary at the upper end of the reservoir. Of the three, we rank the nature center as the most impressive. Also, this is where you can get the best information about nature and hiking. Thus we use the nature center as our point of reference.

Green Lane Reservoir is also an excellent canoeing site. As featured in our *Quiet Water Canoe Guide: Pennsylvania* (published by the AMC), the 805-acre reservoir snakes about 4.5 miles northward from its dam in Green Lane, wandering into numerous coves, inlets, and fingers along the way. Hiking and equestrian trails parallel much of the shoreline.

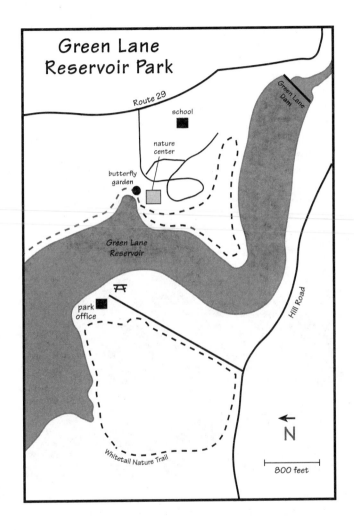

Green Lane Reservoir Park

Route 29

school

nature center

butterfly garden

Green Lane Dam

Green Lane Reservoir

park office

Hill Road

Whitetail Nature Trail

N

800 feet

Nature Center

Open 8:00 A.M. to 4:00 P.M. daily, the Green Lane Reservoir Nature Center features a spectacular butterfly garden. At its peak in mid-summer, the garden attracts many different butterfly and moth species with purple coneflower, Queen Anne's lace, milkweeds, joe-pye weed, black-eyed Susan, yarrow, bee balm, blazing star, butterfly weed, boneset, ironweed, garden phlox, bergamot, and more. We watched a hummingbird (or sphinx) moth working stalks of *Monarda* (bee balm).

Our first encounter with hummingbird moths dates back to the mid-1970s on the shore of Lake Powell in northern Arizona. And at first, like everyone else, we

A hummingbird moth sips nectar from bee balm at the nature center at Green Lane Reservoir Park.

were confused. Scott thought he had spotted one of the many hummingbirds that inhabit the southwestern US. But a quick survey of our field guides introduced us to a curious group of insects called sphinx moths.

Most are active at dusk and after dark, when they sip the nectar of tubular flowers that remain open at night. In return for the meal, the moths pollinate the flowers. The "beak" is actually a long, flexible tube that stays coiled under the head when the moth is not feeding.

Two species are most likely to be seen in Pennsylvania. Both are a bit smaller than hummingbirds but quite large for moths. The white-lined sphinx has a long white line extending the length of its front wings and a rosy-colored stripe across the rear wing. Its heavy brown body tapers to a point at each end and has a series of dark bands across its abdomen. This is the species that visits our petunia bed each evening in the summer.

The other common local species is best known by the name of its caterpillar and is probably more familiar to readers who garden. Tomato hornworms, those fat, green, fleshy caterpillars that eat your tomatoes and their leaves, eventually transform into five-spotted hawkmoths. Adult tomato hornworms are large, gray moths with wingspans of about 4 inches. A series of five or six bright orange spots on each side of the abdomen help identify them.

Larval hornworms are called hornworms because of the soft, spinelike "horn" that projects upward from the rear end of the body. Though the spine looks like a stinger, it's quite harmless. When alarmed, hornworms erect themselves in a stiff, sphinxlike pose—hence the general name of this group of moths.

A tomato hornworm has eight V-shaped white marks on its sides, and its horn is black. Other species are marked differently and may have different-colored horns.

If you find hornworms covered with tiny white capsules in your garden, be relieved not alarmed. These white objects are pupal cases of tiny wasps that parasitize hornworms and control their numbers. They are harmless to people. By the time these pupae hatch, the hornworm will be dead. The larval wasps consumed the hornworm from the inside before emerging to pupate.

The nature center hosts free nature programs every summer weekend. Most are walks or wades. (The reservoir is just yards away.) Hikers use the equestrian trails behind the nature center, as we did one hot, muggy morning in July. From behind the center, we walked down to the lake and turned left to follow the shoreline. (You can turn right and hike along a much longer horse trail.) After following the shore a short distance we came to a fork and headed left to loop back to the nature center. More-ambitious hikers on a cooler day could continue following the shoreline for miles on trails that parallel the shoreline.

Cicadas droned as we walked through the second-growth deciduous forest. Huge beech trees, white oaks, and elms predominated. We encountered many spiderwebs spanning the narrow trail, several complete with entangled flies.

Despite the heat, we saw a downy woodpecker excavating a meal, a broad-winged hawk soaring overhead, and the ubiquitous red-eyed vireo, which seemed to follow us the entire way. We also noticed small pieces of broken glass all along the trail, although there were no other signs of human disturbance.

The best feature of the walk, we decided, was the fungi that littered the trail. We saw many different kinds, all probably owing their existence to the horses that travel these trails and leave their droppings. One word of warning: do not eat wild mushrooms; many are deadly.

Another interesting find was several Indian pipe plants. These curious ghostly white plants lack chlorophyll. Rather than converting sunlight into food, Indian pipe is saprophytic. It extracts its nutritional needs from dead organic matter. Indian pipe grows 6 to 10 inches high, appears waxy, and has a scaly stem.

The trail map we were using indicated that the trail would loop back to the nature center, but we discovered that it actually emerges at an adjacent school. We simply turned left at the school and walked about 100 yards toward the nature center sign. Once inside the gate, we turned left to the parking lot, passing a large picnic area on the way.

In addition to a trail map, ask for a reservoir bird list and a flora guide before hiking here or anywhere in this park.

Whitetail Nature Trail at the Park Office

The park maintains an excellent self-guided, 1-mile loop trail that begins by the office parking lot. An accompanying brochure, which can be obtained at the office, provides a thorough explanation of twenty different stations along the trail.

The trail starts out as a wide graveled path along the lake. It soon cuts back into the woods along an intermittent feeder stream and becomes a narrow dirt footpath. Hemlocks, mixed hardwoods, and beech trees abound.

Accompanied by the musical interludes of a wood thrush and a red-eyed vireo, we followed the gradually ascending trail, which became rocky and littered with exposed tree roots. We stumbled more than a few times. Ferns and slugs seem to love this dark, damp environment.

Look for the huge, old tulip poplar on the right at the top of the hill. Another notable tree is the old white oak at Station 18.

The upper portion of the trail parallels Hill Road through a muddy, overgrown field. Here we encountered remnant eastern red cedars, catbirds, and lots of biting horseflies. Their razor-sharp mouthparts are perfectly adapted for slicing unprotected skin.

The trail emerges at the top of the entrance road. Just follow the road down the hill to the parking lot.

Church Road Bird Sanctuary

The sanctuary is located in the reservoir's upper, marshy reaches, where the Perkiomen Creek feeds into the lake. It provides refuge for waterfowl, waders, and shorebirds. Eagles are sometimes spotted here, as are herons, wood ducks, and other birds. Make sure you take binoculars. We always set up a spotting scope, too. This is an undeveloped area. From the parking lot, you can walk along the water's edge and along the road to reach the best viewing spot. Spring and fall are the best times for viewing migratory shorebirds and waterfowl. Call the nature center to find out the most recent information on species spotted at the sanctuary.

We like to visit during spring migration, from mid-April through early June. During this time we've seen common loons, double-crested cormorants, great egrets, herons, ducks of all types, osprey, bald eagles, plovers, yellowlegs, sandpipers, terns, rails, purple martins, red-headed woodpeckers, and a variety of warblers. Local birding enthusiasts keep a daily bird list at the nature center.

Getting There

The nature center is located behind an elementary school just off Rte. 29, 2.5 miles south of Red Hill or 1.0 mile north of Green Lane and the dam. To get to the main park office, take Rte. 29 south from the nature center for 0.7 mile, then turn right (west) onto Hill Road. Drive another 1.1 miles to the park entrance on the right. To get to the sanctuary, take Rte. 29 north to its intersection with Rte. 663 in Pennsburg (about 5 miles north of the nature center). Turn left (south) and drive 2.0 miles on Rte. 663 to Kutztown/Knight Road (at second light). Turn right and drive 0.2 mile, turn right again onto Church Road, and drive 0.6 mile to a parking area on the right. (To take a shortcut from the sanctuary to the park office, travel south on Rte. 663 from the light at Knight Road for 1.6 miles, then turn left onto Hill Road. The park office is several miles in on the left.)

Facilities: Main office with rowboat rentals, picnic area, portable toilets, large parking lot. Equestrian trails and trailer parking area across the street from office. Nature center at a nearby location with restrooms, picnic area, parking lot. No facilities except a parking lot at the sanctuary.

For More Information: Call 215-234-4863.

Toads

Shortly after sunset each evening the dusk-to-dawn light turns on. Within minutes, insects swarm the illuminated area—lacewings, beetles, assorted true bugs, and more kinds of moths than I'll ever learn to recognize.

Soon bats join the congregation of flying insects. For hours they patrol that corner of the house, gorging themselves on a made-to-order smorgasbord. Perhaps they feed all night; I've never stayed up to watch.

On the ground another visitor—a toad—regularly helps itself to the crawling and low-flying insects the outdoor light attracts. But it's much less conspicuous than the insects or the bats. In silence, it waits patiently for a meal to venture too close. Then, zap! A flash of a deceptively long, sticky tongue and another moth disappears into its mouth.

A toad is a remarkable eating machine. Because it has no teeth and a slow, awkward hopping style, a toad relies on patience to fill its belly. If you doubt that patience works, just watch one for about 30 minutes. It grabs something every few minutes. If it takes a break, it's more likely due to a sated appetite than an inability to catch prey.

American toads inhabit virtually every backyard in the East, even in cities. They spend their days under stairs, rocks, logs, tall grass, or in burrows—places where the air is cool and relatively moist. They emerge nightly in search of food. This is when you'll most likely find them.

After watching for awhile, pick the toad up and examine it. Remember, it has no teeth, so it cannot bite. Study the rather rough, warty skin. Because their skin is thicker than most other amphibian skin, toads can wander and live hundreds of yards from the pools, ponds, and puddles in which they were born. Except for the springtime reproductive season, toads live a mostly terrestrial life.

In March and April males return to their ancestral ponds and puddles and attract females with a loud, melodious trilling song. By inflating the balloonlike vocal sac found under the throat, males increase the volume and resonance of their call. When a female approaches, the pair couples, and the male fertilizes the gelatinous string of eggs the female secretes. She may lay as many as 25,000 eggs.

Under the ideal conditions of a warm spring, the eggs and tadpoles develop rapidly. Toadlets may be found as early as mid-May.

If you handle a toad, it may urinate. But don't worry. Neither toad urine nor their glandular secretions cause warts in humans. That's an old wives' tale. If toads really caused warts, I would have made tabloid headlines as "The

Incredible Wart Boy." When I was a kid, toads were one of my favorite collectibles.

Most predators learn quickly to avoid toads. It takes only one distasteful encounter. The warts that cover the relatively thick skin of toads are clumps of swollen poison glands. The most prominent are called the paratoids and are located behind the eyes on either side of the neck.

The toxin in these glands is strong enough to sicken almost any predator that takes a toad into its mouth. Small dogs can even die if they swallow a mouthful. That's why most predators learn quickly to avoid these foul-tasting insect eaters. Hognose snakes, which are apparently immune to the toxin, are one of the few predators that regularly eat toads.

Though a toad's glandular poison does not cause warts, it can irritate the mucous membranes in your eyes or nose. So be sure to wash your hands after handling a toad.

When your study session is over, return the toad to the place you found it. Or put it in the garden. A toad's appetite alone is enough to earn your respect and hospitality.

13. Evansburg State Park
Evansburg

Hours: Daily, 8:00 A.M. to sunset

The 3,349-acre Evansburg State Park **stretches close to 10 miles along both sides of Skippack Creek.** Human history in the area is long and varied. When William Penn purchased this land in 1684, it was inhabited by the Unami of the Delaware Nation. (Skippack comes from the Delaware Lenape word Skippauhacki, meaning "wetland.") Soon afterwards, German Mennonite settlers began farming the Skippack Valley, and traces of their mills and homesteads still stand.

One such homestead, built by Paul Friedt around 1725, serves as the park's visitor center. Here, visitors can view the house and learn about the people who lived there for 190 years. One exhibit room features displays of local plants and animals. Behind the house, an herb and wildflower garden attracts people, hummingbirds, and butterflies alike. The garden, tended faithfully by two local women, is a German four-square garden of early 1800s vintage. It includes vegetables, herbs, and such flowers as phlox, roses, coreopsis, and foxglove. This garden also serves as the trailhead for a 0.5-mile, self-guided nature trail.

The nature trail is just a small part of the more than 6 miles of hiking trails, but we feel that it's a "must see." Trail markers offer interesting information about the

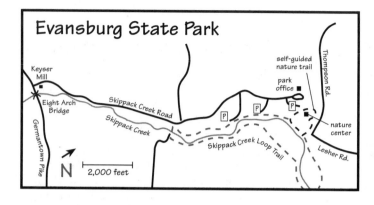

Evansburg State Park

Keyser Mill

Eight Arch Bridge

Skippack Creek Road

Skippack Creek

Germantown Pike

self-guided nature trail

Thompson Rd.

park office ■

P P P

Skippack Creek Loop Trail

nature center ■

Lesher Rd.

N   2,000 feet

area's natural and human history. The trail bisects an area formerly under cultivation, but today it's a beautiful example of ecological succession as the vegetation reverts back to deciduous forest. The trail guide (available at the visitor center) and trail markers point out areas where the Friedt family tended crops and cut hay. At one point along the trail, you can barely make out the remnants of a spring house. (It's much easier to see when the leaves aren't on the trees.)

From behind the visitor center the trail crosses a wooden bridge over a ravine and becomes a narrow dirt footpath. Soon you come to a footbridge over a small run. At an unmarked fork, bear right. Here, we came upon some wooden bat houses that, unfortunately, had been vandalized. Past the bat houses, the trail passes through a weedy, overgrown field. The trail itself is weedy and overgrown and lined with poison ivy.

Eventually the trail comes to Skippack Creek, where it intersects with Skippack Creek Loop Trail. The park area once had seven waterwheel-powered mills along the creek. One good example is the Keyser Mill, which you can see along Skippack Creek Road just north of Germantown Pike and the Eight Arch Bridge.

Turn right onto the Skippack Creek Trail to loop back to the Friedt Homestead and visitor center. You'll cross another footbridge over the same run you crossed a while back. Notice the "brownstone" prevalent in the creek bed. This hard sandstone was used for building materials in early days. We paused along the trail to scan the creek for signs of wildlife. We heard the rattling call of a kingfisher, and sure enough, we soon spotted the bird diving into the creek. We watched it make two unsuccessful dives before it moved farther upstream. While watching it go, two mallard ducks caught our eye, lazily paddling downstream along the opposite bank. In the binoculars, the male's bright green head shined brightly in the morning sun. Following the ducks with the binoculars, we noticed a tall, statuesque creature come into our field of view. A great blue heron had apparently been there the whole time we'd been scanning the creek. Whether is was fishing intently or just hoping to avoid notice, we never did learn, for it didn't moved the entire time we watched.

At the next fork, turn right and climb a small hill to complete the Nature Trail Loop.

Skippack Creek Trail continues left, making a 5-mile loop along both sides of the creek. Watch for the white diamond blazes. You can park and access the trail at both ends, either at the Henry Pennepacker Mill Site on Skippack Creek Road or at the Stone Bridge about 2 miles east. Another good access point is the parking lot near the playground on May Hill Road, south of the park office. Find the trailhead at the end of the loop turn-around. This is also the trailhead for the Mill Race Trail, which overlaps the Skippack Creek Loop Trail for part of its 1-mile distance. Mill Race is an easy, fairly level trail suitable for young and old alike. It passes through deciduous forest and a forty-year-old pine plantation. Mill Race Trail also features a dark, gloomy hemlock grove that one park employee calls a "Hansel and Gretel woods." Our girls agreed with her assessment. Emma pointed out that instead of following bread crumbs along this trail, we were following blue dots painted on trees.

Skippack Creek Loop Trail is longer and a little more rugged, but still suitable for children accustomed to hik-

Nora and Emma take a break.

ing, such as our five-year-old Emma. As its name implies, this trail overlooks the creek for most of its 5 miles. Perhaps most notable are the beautiful spring wildflowers and the ostrich ferns lining this trail. Nora and Emma enjoyed the several chances they had to dip their hot feet in the cool creek. While swimming is not allowed, no one discourages a wade in the foot-deep water.

Be sure to secure a trail map before you hike. And be aware that the Hemlock Slope section of the trail is steep.

Despite its proximity to Norristown, Collegeville, and the densely populated suburbia surrounding Philadelphia, Evansburg State Park is underused, according to park employees. Apparently, many suburbanites are looking for a swimming pool. But that's okay with us. In fact, it's one of the many reasons this park is such a desirable place to visit. We passed fewer than ten people on the several miles of trails we hiked.

One beautiful site visited even less frequently is a picnic area at the park's extreme southwest corner. A short Overlook Trail follows a ridge overlooking a bend in the creek. The trail, about 0.5 mile round-trip, starts at the southwest end of the playing field.

In addition to hiking trails, the park offers 15 miles of equestrian trails. Horseback riding is also allowed on public roads through the park (use the right-side berm).

Finally, if you visit the park in late spring or summer, look for the butterfly garden near the park office. Among the species attracted by a multitude of colorful flowering plants are fritillaries, monarchs, swallowtails, red admirals, and mourning cloaks.

Getting There

From Germantown Pike, about 6 miles northwest of Norristown, turn east (right) onto Skippack Creek Road. Drive 1 mile to the visitor center entrance.

Facilities: Picnic areas, charcoal grills, ball fields, a golf course, comfort stations, park office, youth hostel, and visitor center.

Best Time to Visit: Any time. Summer holiday weekends are most crowded.

Special Note: Poison ivy is prevalent in this park, so take precautions. Also the visitor center hours are sometimes erratic, depending upon whether or not the director is working with a visiting group. Sometimes the door is locked, so make sure you knock before leaving disappointed. Check at the park office (Monday through Friday, 8:00 A.M. to 4:00 P.M.) if you have no luck at the visitor center.

For More Information: Call the park office at 610-489-3729.

Nearby Attractions: This historically rich area features many attractions, including Skippack Village, Valley Forge National Historical Park, and the Audubon Wildlife Sanctuary (Mill Grove). On Germantown Pike, which bisects the park's southwest end, stands the nation's oldest bridge in continuous heavy use. This eight-arch stone bridge was built in 1792 to span Skippack Creek.

14. Riverbend Environmental Education Center
Lower Merion Township

Hours: Dawn to dusk, daily

The privately run Riverbend Environmental Education Center encompasses 28 acres in Lower Merion Township, Montgomery County. Except for the constant hum of traffic from the nearby Schuylkill Expressway, the center has the look and feel of a **private rural estate.** And that's just what it was, until 22 years ago, when it was deeded to the Riverbend Refuge, Inc., for the purpose of preserving undeveloped space for wildlife.

Riverbend gets its name from the 90-degree bend in the Schuylkill River known as Conshohocken Curve. Most popular with the schoolchildren and summer day campers who visit each year, the center also attracts families and casual hikers and nature lovers like us. On a hot, muggy August afternoon we explored 2 miles of interconnecting trails. Starting just behind the barn (headquarters) on the Valley View Trail, we passed the center's amphitheater and intersected with the Aloha Trail just a short distance later. (The Aloha Trail is named for the three-story stone house, called Aloha, which graced the original estate and still stands on the center's edge.)

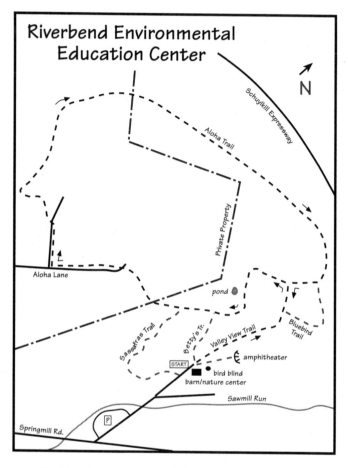

Riverbend Environmental Education Center

Schuylkill Expressway

N

Aloha Trail

Private Property

Aloha Lane

pond

Sassafras Trail

Betty's Tr.

Valley View Trail

Bluebird Trail

START

amphitheater

bird blind

barn/nature center

Sawmill Run

P

Springmill Rd.

Bearing left onto the Aloha Trail we passed some benches, turned left again, and crossed a short field, passing a cattail pond. Here the trail narrowed, and it seemed to be a mowed path through thickets and grapevines. We forked right at an unmarked intersection and shortly emerged onto a paved road. Turning left (and following our trail guide) we passed a giant red oak tree on the right and walked toward several homes. At a trail sign we turned right at the first driveway, passed a house and a tennis court, and turned left again (at a trail sign) into a woods characterized by large elms, tulip poplars, and oaks. The trail, a mere footpath through this wooded section, sloped downhill past a giant beech tree. The traffic noise became almost deafening at this point, as the path parallels the Schuylkill Expressway just 100 or 200 yards away. Giant tulip poplars are the most interesting biological feature.

All other understory growth seems to be choked out by a thick blanket of akebia, a noxious, nonnative, climbing ground cover that outcompetes native species. You can identify it by its five oblong leaflets and purple flower. This is an excellent example of what happens when humans tamper with the natural balance. Unfortunately, center staff report that akebia is widely available at nurseries and garden centers, even though it is essentially unused by native wildlife and can kill the trees if it reaches the canopy level. Center staff and volunteers regularly "free a tree" by cutting out the akebia where it is reaching upward. Gradually they are reclaiming the forest and open areas.

After about 0.25 mile through the woods, the trail cuts back up the hillside to the Valley View Spur again, passing the Bluebird Trail, a tiny spur that joins the Valley View Trail. The Bluebird Trail area was once covered with mile-a-minute, another imported noxious weed.

Poison ivy—leaflets three, let it be!

But center staff have successfully eradicated this pest. Now bluebird boxes dominate the area.

One interesting human artifact on the Riverbend Center property is the old stone fences along the entrance road and along the path leading to the barn and nature center.

The Riverbend Environmental Education Center hosts numerous programs and events, including school classes, guided nature walks, teacher workshops, day camps, Scout programs, family programs, outreach programs, and more. Call for details (610-527-5234).

Getting There

From the Blue Route, take the Conshohocken exit and follow signs for 0.8 mile to Rte. 23. At the Rte. 23 intersection, turn right (east) and drive 1.0 mile, passing one traffic light and coming to another. At the second light, turn left onto Springmill Road (there's a sign for the center). Follow Springmill Road until it ends in 1.0 mile, just past the Philadelphia Country Club, then turn left at the center's sign and entrance.

Facilities: Two miles of interconnecting trails, restrooms, a small nature center in a converted 1923 Sears & Roebuck catalog barn, a reference and children's library, bird blind, and amphitheater.

Best Time to Visit: Weekends and anytime in mid- to late June. Avoid weekday mornings during school, and be aware that day camps run from 9:00 A.M. to 3:30 P.M. in July and August.

Special Note: The center conducts free nature programs on Saturdays at 10:00 A.M. and 2:00 P.M. Call for a schedule.

For More Information: Call the center at 610-527-5234.

Nearby Attractions: Philadelphia Zoo.

Delaware County

15. Ridley Creek State Park
Media

Hours: Daily, 8:00 A.M. to sunset

Natural history and human history intertwine at Ridley Creek State Park to provide a fascinating experience for visitors. The 2,606-acre park, located in Delaware County **just 16 miles from center city Philadelphia,** features 12 miles of hiking trails that crisscross and connect several historic sites.

Popular with many walkers, joggers, and bicyclists is a 5-mile paved, multipurpose trail. Mud and deer ticks can be avoided here because you don't have to walk through the brush. This trail is especially nice for strollers and wheelchairs.

We sought out the less-frequented dirt trails. These trails offer the solitude and birding opportunities we value. Twelve miles of intersecting trails offer many possible combinations and trail lengths. We chose a comfortable 2-mile hike from Picnic Area #16, east of the park office off Sandy Flash Drive South.

The White Trail starts just behind the comfort station. A pretty little garter snake at the trailhead was a good omen that we'd see lots of wildlife. And we did.

Immediately we entered a heavily wooded, fairly mature area. A monstrous tulip poplar tree graced the trail about 0.1 mile in. In late spring you can identify this

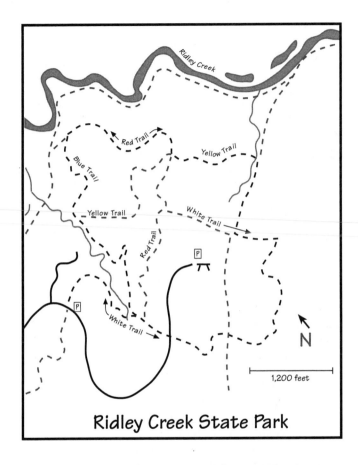

Ridley Creek State Park

tree by its tulip-shaped leaves and flowers. The droning cicadas on a hot summer morning helped to drown out the traffic noise, which early on was noticeable.

After about 0.25 mile, the trail starts to climb a fairly steep hill. At the top, the trail crosses a paved road and continues on through mixed hardwood forest. Just past the road, the trail forks left at a set of wooden steps. Here, the trail widens, offering better birding opportunities. About a hundred yards in from the steps, Scott did his screech owl imitation, and responding within minutes were an American redstart, northern oriole, robin, yellow-throated warbler, rufous-sided towhee, tufted titmouse, white-eyed vireo, white-breasted nuthatch, black-capped chickadee, catbird, a female scarlet tanager, and a cardinal.

The trail proceeds to a stone bridge on the paved multiuse trail. Here we turned right and walked about 0.25 mile, passing an old abandoned homestead (look, don't touch) and a grove of large beech trees.

Next we turned right onto the Blue Trail, a wide, wood-chip trail that loops back to the White Trail and Picnic Area # 16. After crossing the paved road again, we continued through an area of tall shrubs, vines, and young trees, obviously the remnants of old fields. An old sickle mower alongside the trail and an abandoned Colonial stone farmhouse, reminders of yesteryear, are slowly being reclaimed by the encroaching forest. By this time, the trail is a narrow footpath.

Shortly after the farmhouse the Blue Trail intersects with the White Trail at a huge fallen tree. We turned onto the White Trail and walked a short distance to our starting point, hearing and observing an Acadian flycatcher along the way. Its distinctive, unmusical song, "PEET-sa!" is easy to recognize and, like all flycatchers, it makes short flights from open perches to catch flying insects. Its common name refers to Acadia, the French name for

Emma's ready to hit the bike trail.

Nova Scotia, thus implying a northern distribution. The northern limits of the Acadian flycatcher's range, however, extend only to southern New England.

Hiking trails intersect all over the park, so hikers can custom-design a walk of any length or type. One hike we're planning for a return trip is through the Sycamore

Mills Historic District, the remnants of an eighteenth-century village centered around a gristmill on Ridley Creek. This area, which is on the National Register of Historic Places, can be reached via the multipurpose trail from the parking area at the end of Chapel Hill Road, just past the intersection with Bishop Hollow Road (southeast corner of the park). Visitors can still see the miller's house, the office and library, and several mill-workers' dwellings. An informational brochure is available at the park office.

The park's major historic attraction is the Colonial Pennsylvania Plantation, a working farm located in the park's northwest corner, near the Rte. 3 (West Chester Pike) entrance. Here, for a fee, visitors can see a re-created Quaker farm from before the American Revolution. On weekends from April through November, costumed historical interpreters perform regular farm and household chores and crafts. (Call 215-566-1725 for more information.)

Even the park office is a historical structure. Located in the Hunting Hill Mansion built in 1914, the actual visitor reception area is a 1789 Pennsylvania stone farmhouse around which the present mansion was erected.

Getting There

From the intersection of Rtes. 202 and 3, travel east on Rte. 3 for 7.0 miles, then turn right into the park entrance at the park sign (obscured by vegetation). If approaching from the east, closer to Philadelphia, drive 2.5 miles west of Newtown Square, on Rte. 3, to the park entrance on the left.

Facilities: Ridley Creek features almost a thousand picnic tables in fourteen different areas, charcoal grills, comfort stations, playgrounds, ball fields, a trout-stocked creek, a horse stable and concession, environmental and interpretive programs, and many different wheelchair-accessible facilities.

Best Time to Visit: Any time. Bicyclists and joggers use the 5-mile multipurpose trail heavily during the warmer months, so you may wish to visit during a weekday, if possible.

For More Information: Call Ridley Creek State Park at 601-892-3900. Trail maps are available at the park office.

Nearby Attractions: Tyler Arboretum, also featured in this book, is located adjacent to Ridley Creek. Several park trails connect with Tyler Arboretum trails. Ask at the park office for information on those trails.

16. Tyler Arboretum
Media

Hours: 8:00 A.M. to dusk
Fee: $3 adults, $1 children 3 to 15

While researching this book, we were amazed to discover Tyler Arboretum in an area we thought we knew well. Although born and raised in southeastern Pennsylvania, neither of us had ever heard of this delightful place. It's a **secluded gem in the middle of urban sprawl**, a 650-acre estate crisscrossed with hiking trails through various habitats and types of plantings. The arboretum was established in 1825 when two brothers, Jacob and Minshall Painter, began to plant more than one thousand types of trees and shrubs. The property was offered as a public arboretum in 1944 by Laura Tyler, a direct descendant of Thomas Minshall, who acquired the land from William Penn in 1681.

Exploring Tyler Arboretum can be a pleasant half-day adventure or a full day of hiking and nature watching. Some 20 miles of trails are packed into 450 uncultivated acres, so it's not difficult to imagine how the trails crisscross and weave among each other. It's really impossible to get lost. And it's a good thing, because we found that the trail map was extremely difficult to follow. Also confusing is the trailhead, located behind the visitor center. We couldn't find trail name markers any-

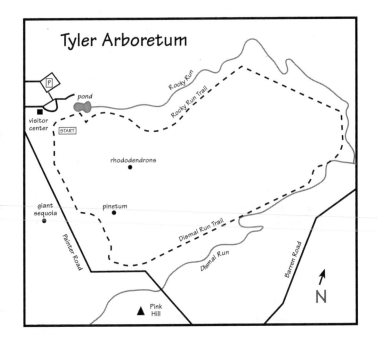

where, so we headed for some blue blaze marks and set out on what our map identified as the Rocky Run Trail.

The dirt trail led through a deciduous woods of hickory, oak, and maple, then over a mowed path through an overgrown pasture, and back into the woods again. Compare the bark of these dominant hardwoods. Hickory bark is rough and shaggy. Oaks are coarse and furrowed. Red maples, a common tree in young forests, have smooth bark much like beeches.

Tyler Arboretum's rich diversity of trees makes it an ideal place to study tree identification. Carry along a field guide to trees and study the common species. Important characteristics distinguishing closely related species include leaf shape and size; bud size, shape, number, and location; blossoms; and color and texture of the bark. It doesn't take much practice to recognize major groups such as oak, hickories, beeches, and maples.

Though oaks and hickories indicate a mature forest, red maples invade moist disturbed areas and are usually understory trees. Their presence indicates a relatively young forest, though they may persist for decades along wet valleys and stream banks. Spring through autumn, red maple earns its name with displays of crimson blooms, fruits, leaf stalks, and fall foliage.

Rocky Run itself is a pretty little rock-strewn stream. The trail crosses the stream several times. We passed only one other couple on a weekday in early August. And as daughter Nora, our trailblazer, can tell you, we encountered many spiderwebs stretched across the lonely trail.

Halfway into our hike we switched over to Dismal Run Trail, ending up at the Giant Sequoia Tree. This state champion tree was brought to the property in 1856 by the Painter brothers. It's located in the Pinetum, an 85-acre planting that includes pines, spruces, firs, cedars, hemlocks, and other evergreens.

Trail surfaces through the woods were usually hard-packed dirt, with some trail portions rockier than others. Sometimes they looked like vehicle trails with heavy polygonum stands growing up between tire tracks.

A tiger swallowtail takes some nectar.

There is also a fair amount of mowed trail through fields. At one such spot we found black raspberry bushes hanging heavy with fruit.

Back at the education center, we noticed lots of class activity. The arboretum offers courses and workshops for teachers, other adults, and children. An events schedule published by the arboretum regularly lists these educational opportunities.

In addition to the hiking trails, visitors can walk around enjoying the many areas of special plantings. These include butterfly and hummingbird gardens, a fragrant garden, and collections of rhododendron, flowering cherry, lilac, magnolia, holly, and crabapple. Endemic wildflowers are featured on Pink Hill. Sketch or photograph the gardens for expert reference material to create similar gardens in your own backyard.

For more information, call 610-566-5431.

Getting There

From US Rte. 1 take Rte. 352 North and drive for 2 miles, passing the Penn State Delaware County campus along the way. Turn right at the sign for Tyler Arboretum and drive 0.5 mile on Painter Road to the arboretum entrance on the left.

Eastern Tent Caterpillars

There is no more ordinary creature than the eastern tent caterpillar. In late April and early May their distinctive silky tents begin to appear in woods, old fields, and along country roads. Yet their life history is as extraordinary and mysterious as any of their lepidopteran kin.

It's hard to know where to begin the story. Tent caterpillars spend most of their lives inside an egg. Adult moths live just a few days. The form we know best, the caterpillar, is the most conspicuous.

Let's fast-forward to late June or early July. A small brown moth struggles free from a cocoon fastened to the inside of a slab of loose bark on an old dying tree. Blood courses through its unfurling wings; within a few hours the 1.5-inch moth is on the wing. It wanders purposefully, led by olfactory cues, in search of a mate. Within 48 hours, the female is bred. Now she searches for apple, cherry, and other fruit trees. She deposits a cluster of two hundred to three hundred eggs around a small twig. Their responsibilities satisfied, adult males and females die just a few days after emerging from the cocoon.

The moth's destiny now lies inside the egg case that hardens on the twig. Through the blistering heat of summer and the frigid cold of winter, the eggs lay dormant, shielded from the elements only by the egg case's thin protective membrane. Thanks to a natural antifreeze called glycerol, which makes up 35 percent of the eggs' weight, by January, the fluids in the embryos remain unfrozen.

Inside the eggs, a biological clock ticks, marking off the months until spring's longer days trigger the clock's alarm. The eggs hatch in April and tiny, hungry caterpillars emerge. They migrate downward toward a centrally located crotch in the tree and begin spinning and weaving the familiar tent. The caterpillars work in shifts to build a shelter that consists of many horizontal layers, not unlike a dish of lasagna or baklava. The space between each layer is just large enough to accommodate a group of caterpillars.

When not resting or building the tent, tent caterpillars march upward along the tree's smallest branches in search of fresh tender leaves. They eat voraciously and grow rapidly. To ensure that they can find their way back to the tent, tent caterpillars leave behind a trail of silk. The combined efforts of the colony yield an extensive network of silky trails that always lead home. If Hansel and Gretel had been so skilled, the Brothers Grimm would have had one less fairy tale to tell.

Insect growth is limited by an elastic exoskeleton that can stretch only so far. It then splits, and the old exoskeleton is shed. Tent caterpillars molt six times from April through June. Each time hormones control the process to ensure that a new, larger caterpillar, rather than a premature moth, results.

After the final molt, the concentration of juvenile hormone ebbs so that when the mature caterpillar attains a certain critical weight, the next transformation is far more dramatic. At this critical size, other hormones kick in. Caterpillars lose their appetite and wander in search of a place to pupate. This is when we see them crossing roads, trails, and lawns.

Under a log, a rock, or a slab of bark, the tent caterpillar undergoes its final and most miraculous transformation. First, it weaves itself a silky cocoon, being careful to leave a weak spot from which its final incarnation can emerge. Over the course of the next three weeks, the caterpillar physiologically and biochemically transforms itself from hairy caterpillar to scale-covered moth.

Adult moths have a single purpose—reproduction. That done, the short-lived moths die, and a new generation of eggs awaits the following spring. It's an extraordinary story for such an ordinary creature.

17. Brandywine River Trail
Chadds Ford

Hours: Dawn to dusk year-round

The Brandywine River Trail starts at the Brandywine River Museum, a restored nineteenth-century gristmill that showcases the paintings of three generations of Wyeths. The trail follows the slow-moving, languid Brandywine for several hundred yards, then cuts across a wetlands area to open meadows and fields, where it ends at the historic John Chadds House. This is the **beautiful countryside that inspired the Wyeths** and other Delaware County artists—a countryside that also experienced Revolutionary War battles and now features some of the most culturally and historically exciting sites in the Philadelphia area.

The trail passes under and stays close by busy US Rte. 1, but on the hazy August morning we visited, the cicadas almost drowned out the traffic noise. It was easy to forget for a time the people and places nearby.

The trailhead is right behind the museum building, easily accessible from the parking lot. It's graveled at the beginning but soon gives way to a dirt path lined by giant, gnarled maples. The path closely hugs the river, and our girls found frequent spots to sit on a tree trunk or exposed root out over the water. At one such spot, as we sat to observe and cool off, we noticed a shed snake-skin wrapped along a tree branch about 20 feet off the

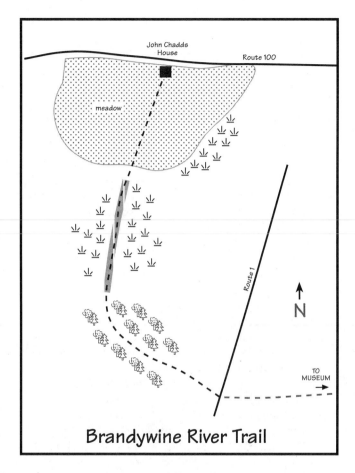

Brandywine River Trail

ground. Looking closer with binoculars, we soon noticed the head of a large black rat snake itself peeking from a nearby hole. Rat snakes are excellent climbers and often eat eggs and chicks found in active nests.

Soon we passed under the US Rte. 1 bridge. On the other side, a power line cuts through the woods, and the vegetation is young and periodically cut back.

Just after the power line, the trail veers right and proceeds along a boardwalk for more than 400 yards. We passed through thick stands of cattails, sedges, swamp willow, multiflora rose, water lilies, ironweed, joe-pye weed, goldenrod, and other wetland plants. From a viewing area in the middle of the boardwalk, we spied red-winged blackbirds, indigo buntings, common yellowthroats, song sparrows, and myriad dragonflies and damselflies. There have also been reports of wood ducks, black ducks, and osprey in this area. Raccoons use the boardwalk, too; we had to watch for raccoon droppings as we made our way along the walkway.

Apparently, this wetland was historically an oxbow loop along the Brandywine. Oxbows form when nearly complete loops in meandering streams and rivers get cut off from the main stream during floods, creating a new watercourse. The original oxbow floods during high water, thus maintaining the wet nature of the area, but it is no longer part of the stream. Over time, usually measured in decades or centuries, this is one way streams and rivers change their paths.

The boardwalk ends at the edge of a meadow. It's just 100 yards or so across the open meadow to Rte. 100 and the John Chadds House. Meadowlarks and red-winged blackbirds nest in the meadow, and the prolific swamp milkweed at the meadow's edge attracts countless butterflies—fritillaries, skippers, several types of swallowtails, and monarchs. We also saw bluebirds on the fence posts and chimney swifts soaring overhead. The John Chadds House was closed during our visit (it's open weekends or by appointment), but we explored the grounds a bit and found an herb garden behind a spring-house and a little duckweed-covered pond on the edge of the meadow. Duckweed is one of the smallest flowering plants in North America, and tens of thousands of these tiny plants often cover small ponds like a carpet. It provides excellent camouflage for frogs, which are quite common in small ponds.

The entire walk took us less than 60 leisurely minutes on a hot day, but it was a welcome respite from our touring in the area. It's a great walk to combine with other

A bullfrog surfaces amid the duckweed in a small pond.

nearby attractions, such as the Brandywine River Museum, the Brandywine Battlefield, or Longwood Gardens.

Back at the parking lot we spent several minutes admiring the joe-pye weed just brimming with butterflies and the parking lot light poles thickly covered in trumpet creeper. They're both part of the perennial wildflower and native plant gardens maintained by the Brandywine Conservancy. A brochure about the gardens identifies plant species and serves as a seasonal guide.

You may be able to obtain a guide to the River Trail at the museum's front desk. If none is available, the information is printed on a kiosk at the trailhead.

For more information, call the Brandywine River Museum at 610-388-2700.

Getting There

Located in Chadds Ford just south of the junction of US Rte. 1 and PA Rte. 100, about 28 miles southwest of Philadelphia and 12 miles north of Wilmington, DE.

Nearby Attractions: In addition to the Brandywine River Museum, the Brandywine Valley features many historical and cultural attractions. Two within just a few miles of the River Trail are Longwood Gardens (610-388-6741) and Brandywine Battlefield Park (610-459-3342). For more information on the cultural and historical opportunities in Delaware County call the Convention and Visitors Bureau at 800-343-3983.

Chester County

18. White Clay Creek Preserve
Newark, Delaware

Hours: 8:00 A.M. to sunset

Straddling the border of Pennsylvania and Delaware in southern Chester County, just 3 miles north of Newark, Delaware, White Clay Creek Preserve is a 1,253-acre tract that originally belonged to William Penn. Penn bought the land in 1683 from Lenapi Indian Chief Keke-lappen. The preserve was once the site of a large Native American village where Kekelappen probably lived. (Archaeologists estimate that native peoples lived in the White Clay Creek Valley for 12,000 years.) The du Pont Company donated the land in 1984 to Pennsylvania and Delaware as a preserve.

White Clay Creek Preserve features many different and unique plants and animals. It also contains several important historical sites. Where once the native village stood, a prosperous milling and agricultural community thrived in the eighteenth and nineteenth centuries.

From the historic Chambers-Folwell Visitor Center in the Delaware portion of the park, we took the 2.1-mile Nature Trail Loop. The first part of the trail follows White Clay Creek to the Pennsylvania state line. In mid-

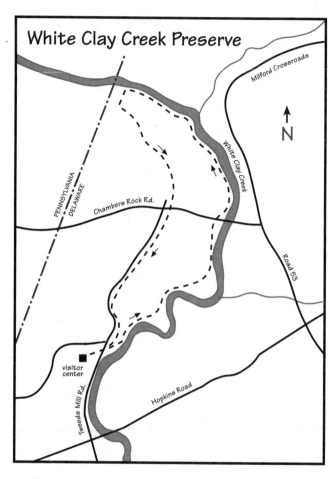

White Clay Creek Preserve

July, the creek appeared to be a popular swimming area. We passed several different groups of swimmers along the way.

A giant red oak tree and **many huge beech and sycamores dot the floodplain** along the trail. This is a great place to compare the barks of these three common trees, especially when leaves are off the trees in winter. Red oak bark is deeply furrowed, suggesting an image of long vertical ski tracks. Beech bark is gray and smooth. Sycamore bark is white, and it flakes off older trees in large pieces.

Farther along, the stream flowed faster, and we came upon a person lying face-down in the riffles, watching fish with the aid of a mask. On a hot summer day, when humidity and biting insects can be overwhelming, there's no better way to cool off than **fish watching.** Belly down in shallow riffles, equipped only with a mask and snorkel, you spy on the colorful world of breeding minnows and darters. In deeper pools, bass gobble crayfish and small frogs and sunfish inhale small fish and aquatic insects. And if you are really patient and still, you might get an underwater view of a kingfisher or heron spearing a fish.

The mature hardwood forest on our left soon gave way to old fields. A juvenile red-tailed hawk screamed in the distance. We stopped for a few minutes to watch a green heron. It perched on a dead log overhanging the creek—a perfect fishing stand. Minutes passed, then its hunched neck exploded to full extension. When it pulled its head from the water, a small water snake dangled from its bill.

The trail intersects a road and a bridge, which appears to be another popular swimming spot. Here, if you bear right and cross the road, you can hike or bike for about 3 miles into the Pennsylvania portion of the

Nora takes care crossing a rocky stream.

preserve, along the east branch of the creek. We opted to turn left onto the hardtop and walked about 200 yards up a slight grade to a gravel trail on the left. This is the other side of the loop, and now we were working our way back to the visitor center.

At first we passed through old fields. Multiflora rose, an invasive exotic species planted in the 1940s and 1950s for its value to wildlife, and grapevine thickets bordered the trail. Soon we saw the screaming red-tailed. Judging from its insistent calls, we speculated that it was probably the first day its parents had stopped feeding it. Perhaps it was protesting its forced independence. We saw several cottontails in the thickets, so the red-tailed would probably not go hungry for long.

About halfway back to the visitor center the trail enters the forest again. Just inside the woods, we stopped by a giant white oak, and Scott did his screech owl call. We were inundated almost immediately by songbirds intent upon scolding and mobbing the "intruder." We identified a black-billed cuckoo, Carolina chickadees, blue-winged warbler, wood thrush, titmice, Acadian flycatcher, cardinal, and red-eyed vireo.

The moment was interrupted by several bicyclists emerging from farther along the trail, and we soon encountered several more. Mostly, the bicyclists confine themselves to the roads in and along the borders of the preserve.

Back at the nature center we took some time to examine the environmentally friendly features—shredded tires used in place of gravel at the kiosk, litterbags provided, and a comfort station with composting toilets. The visitor center itself is an eighteenth century farmhouse. Only one room on the first floor is open to visitors, but it's interesting to examine even from the outside. Various pamphlets and information about the area's natural and cultural history are available inside.

There is no visitor center on the Pennsylvania side, so we recommend you use the Delaware side as your base of operation. There are, however, several historic buildings worth seeing on the Pennsylvania portion. One is the London Tract Baptist Meeting House, built in 1729. The meetinghouse can be toured during limited hours (call ahead). The restrooms built onto the structure are open only when the meetinghouse is. But visitors can wander around the old cemetery any time, looking for the names of the area's eighteenth- and nineteenth-century residents.

Getting There

From the intersection of Rte. 202 and US Rte. 1, drive south on Rte. 1 15.5 miles. Exit at Rte. 841, turn left, and travel south 6.2 miles to Rte. 896. Turn left on Rte. 896 and travel 4.4 miles, then turn left at the preserve sign. Drive another mile to the visitor center on the left. An alternate route is to take the Forrestville exit off Rte. 1 and drive 11.0 miles south on Rte. 896.

For More Information: Call the White Clay Creek Preserve at 215-255-5415 (PA) or the White Clay Creek State Park (DE) at 302-368-6900.

Nearby Attractions: Adjacent to the preserve and just south of the visitor center is the White Clay Creek State Park. Day-use recreational facilities and more than a dozen miles of marked trails are available for a fee. Call 302-368-6900. Also, ask about the Possum Hill Trails, administered by the park—a moderately difficult hike through mature stands of beech and oak.

Berks County

19. Hawk Mountain Sanctuary
Kempton

Hours: Trails open dawn to dusk

Somewhere to the north the broad-winged hawks awoke to a warm September dawn. They were restless. Instinct—ancient genetic instructions—called them south. By journey's end, they would be in South America where lizards and snakes abound during the winter months.

Meanwhile, we sat perched atop Hawk Mountain with a group of dedicated hawk watchers. By 9:00 the morning sun had warmed the surrounding valley, and convection currents of warm air began to climb the mountain wall. As the warmed air rose, cooler air rushed in to replace it, only to also warm and rise. These "thermal" currents (thermals for short) provided the lift that the broad-wings needed to continue their southward journey.

Why flap your wings for thousands of miles when you can ride a series of thermals that will transport you hundreds of miles each day? Birds, and most animals for that matter, often favor efficiency over speed or power.

"Bird!" someone shouted as a dot appeared on the north horizon. Moments later, another identified it,

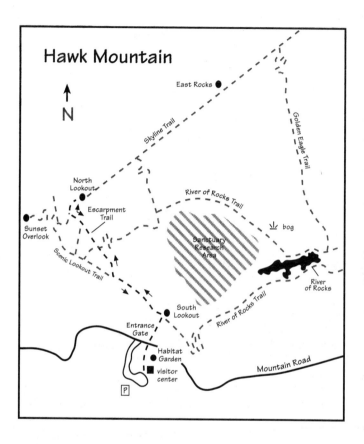

Hawk Mountain

↑
N

East Rocks ●

Skyline Trail

Golden Eagle Trail

North Lookout ●

Escarpment Trail

River of Rocks Trail

⚜ bog

Sunset Overlook ●

Sanctuary Research Area

Scenic Lookout Trail

River of Rocks

South Lookout ●

Entrance Gate

River of Rocks Trail

Habitat Garden ●

■ visitor center

P

Mountain Road

"Broad-wing." A third person clicked a handheld counter, and a fourth recorded the bird on a data sheet.

Slowly the broad-wings moved through—singles, doubles, and small groups of three and four. Three or more broad-wings rising on a thermal are called a "kettle." That day the kettles were small, none more than a half-dozen birds.

Hawk Mountain Sanctuary on a clear, crisp autumn day comes close to heaven—literally and figuratively. From the rocky North Lookout, towering 1,521 feet in the midst of the central Appalachian Mountains, hikers can observe hawks, falcons, and an occasional eagle soaring nearby. The annual fall migration of birds of prey is the sanctuary's claim to fame. Located along a major flyway, the 2,226-acre sanctuary sees an average of 20,000 hawks, eagles, and falcons from mid-August to mid-December. But even if you don't see a single raptor, the scenery alone is well worth the trip. From our perch on the North Lookout we viewed a spectacular panorama of the ridges and valleys below, all in flaming fall colors.

From the parking area and visitor center, cross the highway to reach the entrance gate. Sanctuary association members have free access to trails, but others must pay $4 per person ($3 for seniors, $2 for children 6 to 12). Several hundred yards past the entrance gate is the South Lookout. You may see raptors at this rocky outcrop but not nearly as many as at the North Lookout. If you plan to hike the 0.75 mile to North Lookout, be sure you're wearing sturdy footgear. This means hiking boots, not tennis shoes. This trail is extremely rough and rocky as it ascends 200 feet through oak and hemlock woods. In fall it can be even more treacherous, and we stumbled more than once over rocks and roots hidden by fallen leaves. The few preschoolers we saw along this trail were all being carried by adults. We feel certain that our own five-year-old would have had trouble on this trail. But it's beautiful and well worth the effort for those

Mayapple, a common woodland wildflower, in full bloom. Note the umbrella-like leaves.

who are capable and prepared. In late spring, the mountain laurel understory blooms profusely in pale pink blossoms.

More-ambitious hikers will enjoy other trails in the sanctuary, particularly the 3.5-mile River of Rocks Trail.

Beginning at the South Lookout, the trail drops 600 feet down the mountain to a mile-long boulder field. This rocky "river" formed 11,000 years ago during the last glacial period. As the rocky, exposed ridge tops expanded and contracted during intense cold and freezing, rocks loosened and slid to the valley below. Today, a small stream trickles beneath the river of rocks. This trail is strenuous. Not only are you descending then ascending a mountain, you must walk on rocks and boulders most of the way. It would be easy to lose your footing.

The 2-mile Skyline Trail follows a ridge top from the North Lookout to the East Rocks and beyond to the Appalachian Trail. The Golden Eagle Trail links the River of Rocks Trail and the Skyline Trail. Be sure to pick up a trail map at the entrance gate. The sanctuary's six trails intersect, and you need a map not only for safety reasons but to plan your hiking most efficiently.

The private, nonprofit sanctuary association has set aside 70 percent of its lands for research and an undisturbed wildlife refuge. This research, which has contributed significantly to worldwide raptor conservation, includes the important annual raptor counts. Fall migration counts, first started in 1934, allow researchers to examine population trends and detect declining numbers. For example, Hawk Mountain researchers discovered significantly declining eagle populations in the 1950s, which led to research that uncovered the serious effects of widespread DDT use.

Hawk Mountain is enjoyed by some seventy thousand people annually, many of whom visit during the peak autumn months. For more private trails and a more solitary experience, visit the sanctuary during the week.

You may still encounter one or two high school groups, as we did the October day we visited. But they confine themselves primarily to the North Lookout. Even during peak weekends the trails other than Scenic Lookout Trail are largely ignored. Most people have come to see the raptors. Also, visits during spring or summer have their own rewards—blooming mountain laurel and rhododendron, migrating songbirds, and even some raptors.

For more information call the sanctuary at 610-756-6961.

Getting There

From I-78/US 22 about 25 miles west of Allentown, take Exit 11 at Lenhartsville and turn left onto Rte. 143. Travel north on Rte. 143 through scenic hills and farm country for 4.0 miles, then turn left (unmarked crossroad) at the large, brown Hawk Mountain Sanctuary sign. Travel 6.8 miles (through the village of Albany) to the sanctuary parking area and entrance.

Nearby Attractions: The Pennsylvania Dutch Folklife Museum is located in Lenhartsville, on Rte. 143, just 0.25 mile south of the Exit 11 ramp (turn right at the stop sign instead of turning left toward the sanctuary).

Crystal Cave is a privately run natural attraction located near Kutztown off Rte. 222. The cave is small and the tour is brief, but it houses some spectacular formations. After cooling off in the chilly cave, you can warm up by roaming the nature trails that explore the site's 125 acres.

20. Nolde Forest Environmental Education Center
Reading

Hours: Dawn to dusk from the Sawmill Parking Area; 8:00 A.M. to 4:00 P.M. Monday to Friday at main entrance and mansion.

Despite its proximity to Reading, Nolde Forest **creates the impression of isolation and tranquillity.** Massive white oaks in full red "plumage" and a strong pine smell greeted us at the Nolde Mansion parking lot that sunny, late October morning. As we began our hike, the scrunchy, shuffling sounds of dry oak leaves underfoot easily drowned out the distant hum of motorized vehicles.

This heavily wooded 665-acre tract is a far cry from the clear-cut hills Reading businessman Jacob Nolde found in 1904. He purchased the land and hired a forester to plant an evergreen forest similar to Germany's Black Forest. Later, Jacob's son Hans finished the project his father had started. The state purchased the property in the late 1960s and, by 1970, established Nolde Forest as the first environmental education center operated by the Bureau of State Parks. Today, anyone can enjoy the restored forests and 10 miles of hiking trails.

One of the best hikes, and certainly one we'd recommend, is the Boulevard Trail. Accessible from either

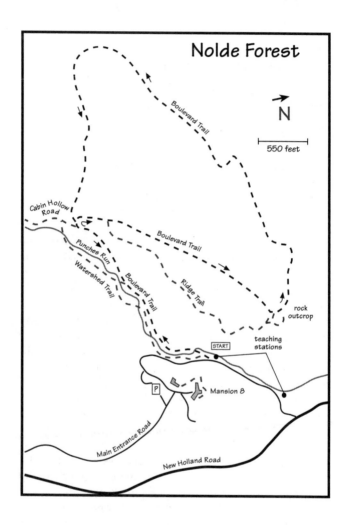

Nolde Forest

N

550 feet

Boulevard Trail

Cabin Hollow Road

Boulevard Trail

Punches Run

Watershed Trail

Boulevard Trail

Ridge Trail

rock outcrop

START

teaching stations

P

Mansion 8

Main Entrance Road

New Holland Road

parking area, the trail begins at the teaching station below the mansion, on the paved walkway joining the two parking areas. If you approach from the mansion parking lot, notice the large beech trees along the road leading down to the trailhead and teaching station. Beech's smooth gray bark is unmistakable and its long pointed buds make identification easy even in mid-winter. In the fall, triangular beechnuts encased in spiny husks cover the ground.

Boulevard Trail is an old fire road that loops 2 miles through hardwood and pine forest. The trail ascends more than 300 feet, but the climb is gradual and trail surfaces are great. We'd rate it an easy, enjoyable walk. Do carry a trail map, however, as you will encounter some unmarked trails. (Unmarked trails that do not appear on the map are no longer maintained, and hikers are discouraged from using them.) In fact, we didn't even see a marker for Boulevard Trail until after we had left the teaching station, crossed an old stone bridge, and proceeded straight ahead for several hundred yards up a hill on a wide, graveled path until we came to a comfort station and fork in the trail. From that point, you can head south on Cabin Hollow Road (which intersects with several other trails) or turn right to continue on Boulevard, which we did. From this point, Boulevard makes a large loop. We chose to travel the loop counterclockwise, making a sharp right turn at the rest station.

Here, the trail levels out for about a half-mile. We were barely past the comfort station when we glimpsed an owl (probably a barred owl) glide silently overhead and land in a nearby tree. Though owls are usually active at night, hikers sometimes startle owls from their daytime roosts. Sharp-eyed hikers will often notice an owl's silent flush. The owl we saw alarmed a pileated woodpecker, who in turn alerted other smaller songbirds. A mob scene ensued as the smaller birds scolded and harassed the bigger owl. After a few minutes, the owl had enough. It flew off into the canopy.

At Nolde Forest, and at most natural areas, the best natural encounters will be those you least expect. Just keep your eyes open and be receptive to the world around you, and you will see some wondrous sights.

Not long after our owl sighting we noticed a buck rub on an old snag: ribbons of bark hung from the sapling where a mature white-tailed deer had rubbed it with his antlers. The rub was a visual signal to other bucks that this area was occupied. And just a bit farther, we noticed a screech owl box in a conifer stand. The small screech owl is fairly easy to attract to man-made nest boxes, even in wooded backyards.

At the far northeast end of the loop lies the Rock Outcrop. This outcrop makes a nice observation and resting area. This area was once the site of a fire tower, but we saw no evidence of it. You can sit on the high rocks and bask in the sun, listening to chipmunks chirping and scurrying nearby. The outcrop lies in a heavily wooded area, so there is no real view here, but it's a beautiful spot nonetheless, especially among the fall colors.

As we continued along the Boulevard Trail and worked our way around the back half of the loop, we encountered only two other hikers. We thought that the absence of human activity on the outer trails (away from the paved trail between the two parking lots) was notable on that warm, sunny Saturday October morning.

Traffic noises sometimes intruded from the urban sprawl nearby, but we were delighted to discover how isolated we could feel this close to Reading. We had fun pretending we were hiking through our own private preserve. And since public lands belong to all of us, we were.

We noticed the high-pitched squeak of a kinglet in a conifer grove just past the Rock Outcrop. We paused to listen. Scott did his screech owl call, and immediately we were mobbed by chickadees, nuthatches, blue jays, titmice, downy woodpeckers, kinglets, robins, a red-bellied woodpecker, and a brown creeper who came to investigate the "intruder." The noise was incredible as dozens and dozens of birds sounded the alarm in reaction to this "predator."

Flowering dogwood in full bloom.

Over the years Scott has found that by imitating the tremulous whistle of the screech owl, he can attract birds into close view. It's almost always successful, but this was the best response he'd ever had. The variety and numbers of birds he attracted attested to the habitat diversity and quality of the Nolde Forest. There are upland and lowland areas, large conifer groves interspersed with tracts of deciduous trees, and even some small, open areas required by certain animal species. We saw two deer along the back half of the trail, and chipmunks scampered everywhere.

Toward the middle of the trail's back-half loop, there is a fairly steep climb to the top of a ridge. There, we encountered many large tulip poplar trees, their golden leaves glowing in the October sun. The trail surface changes in this back half of the loop, too, from gravel to grass and dirt. The entire trail length, however, is well maintained, with smooth, even surfaces.

When you loop back to the comfort station, you can backtrack down the hill on the wide graveled trail to the teaching station and the paved path, or you can take the Watershed Trail, which roughly parallels the Boulevard Trail. We opted for the latter, always looking for new places and discoveries. If you take this return route, be careful not to miss the trail steps on the left side just before the wooden bridge.

The Watershed Trail follows a small stream flowing down the mountain. There is another little teaching center with benches about 200 yards down the trail. Center coordinator Dan Hewko told us later that this trail sports lots of spring wildflowers. There are even pink moccasin flowers (a.k.a., pink lady slippers) now that the deer herd is being managed and controlled. This trail is one of the few built by the state; most of them are simply old fire roads built by the Noldes for access to the various tree plantations.

Nolde Forest accommodates all levels of hiking ability. The paved trail connecting the two parking lots is wheelchair and stroller accessible. Two short loop trails, one at the mansion and one at the sawmill, are also wheelchair accessible. These short trails and others around the mansion and Sawmill Parking Area are wonderful for younger or less abled hikers. You can choose a leisurely 1- or 2-hour hike, as we did. Or you can spend most of the day exploring the entire 10-mile network of trails.

Visitors are welcome to hike, watch wildlife, and take pictures. Bike riding is limited to the main access road, and picnicking is strongly discouraged. Center staff suggest you eat lunch at your car before or after you hike. Picnic areas on the grounds are reserved for school groups and other special groups.

Maps of hiking trails are available at the mansion during the week or at a kiosk in the Sawmill Parking Area. Make sure you carry one, as well as tick repellent in the spring and summer. Populations of deer ticks are high in this area.

If you visit during the week, be sure to see the Tudor-style mansion built by Hans Nolde in the 1920s. This mansion now houses offices, meeting rooms, and a public library featuring resources and materials on pollution, conservation, and other environmental topics. Year-round educational programs are hosted at the mansion.

For more information, call the Nolde Forest Environmental Education Center at 610-775-1411.

Getting There

From US 222 in Reading, 1.0 mile north of Shillington, turn south on Rte. 625 and go 3.4 miles to Nolde Park Office Lane. (You will pass the intersection with Rte. 724 on the way.) Turn right and drive another 0.4 mile to the parking area and historic office building. The gate in this area opens at 8:00 A.M. and closes at 4:00 P.M. Monday through Friday. The Sawmill Parking Area, located 0.8 mile before Nolde Park Office Lane (2.6 miles from Rte. 222), is open from sunrise to sunset daily.

Nearby Attractions: The Reading Outlet Malls are a major nearby landmark; you may coax and unenthusiastic couch-potato spouse into a woodland visit in exchange for a few hours at the malls.

Great Horned Owl: King of the Woods

Shortly after sunset, a cottontail emerged from a snow-covered thicket and hopped to a grove of succulent sumac shoots. It sat motionless and alert for a half-minute, then began stripping bark from the stems. Hungry and intent on its meal, the rabbit relaxed for just a moment.

A great horned owl, perched in a cherry tree about 100 feet away, dropped into the air and sailed silently toward the rabbit. In its final moments the rabbit may have sensed danger—it sat up just before impact. The force of the collision sent the pair tumbling in the snow, but the owl's talons expertly impaled the rabbit's back. There was no struggle.

Near a barn on the edge of the woods a half-mile away, another deadly drama unfolded. In this case, however, the victim was a large rat, and the hunter was the first owl's mate. This one launched its attack from its perch on a power line pole.

It was a good evening. The pair went two for two.

East of the Mississippi River, where wolves and mountain lions were exterminated decades ago, where black bears roam only certain mountainous areas, where bobcats are so secretive their presence goes almost unnoticed, the great horned owl reigns as king of the woods.

I give great horned owls this title because they sit atop the food chain. They eat everything from insects to crows, turkeys, skunks, and other owls, though mice, rats, and rabbits comprise most of their diet. But rarely does anything eat an adult great horned owl. Crows may occasionally grab their eggs or small chicks at an unprotected nest, but most horned owl mortality can be attributed to disease, accidental death, and ignorant fools with nothing better to do than shoot protected birds.

Despite their size—2 feet tall and a wingspan of up to 5 feet—great horned owls often go undetected in the woods. They spend their days perched quietly in conifers or in deciduous trees that cling tenaciously to clumps of dead leaves. And they spread themselves out. A single bird may cover more than a square mile in the course of its daily activities. So your chances of seeing one on a walk in the woods are slim.

In December, adults begin courting and calling. Great horned owls are the "hoot owl" so many people hear, but seldom see. Listen for a series of three to seven simple hoots. A five-syllable call may suggest the phrase, "Don't kill owls, save owls!"

Another part of courtship is selecting the nest, which is often the same one the female used the year before. Great horned owls don't build their own nests; they take over someone else's. Often it's an old red-tailed hawk or crow nest, but occasionally they occupy a large tree cavity.

The female lays the first of her two or three eggs in late January or early February. She lays the eggs at 3-day intervals, but incubation begins immediately with the first egg. This is why you may see photographs of owlets of several sizes in the same nest. The eldest sibling in a brood of three may be 6 days older than the youngest.

Incubation continues for 28 to 34 days, often under a blanket of snow, with the first egg laid being the first to hatch. Both parents take turns warming the eggs.

Young horned owls may remain in the nest for 2 months. Nestlings begin to exercise their wings at 6 weeks but are not proficient fliers until they are about 10 weeks old. Young owls perfect their hunting skills slowly and remain dependent on their parents for food well into fall.

Learning the skills to hunt successfully takes time, but once mastered, nothing in the eastern woods does it better than the great horned owl.

21. French Creek State Park
Elverson

Hours: Daily, 8:00 A.M. to sunset

Plan to spend a full day at French Creek State Park. This park abounds in both **natural and human history,** most of it accessible by foot. Some 32 miles of trails crisscross the park's 7,339 acres. These trails range from less than a mile to more than 8 miles. Be sure to get a trail guide and reliable current information at the park office before setting out on some of the longer, more remote trails.

We recommend three distinct "adventures" here: a hike around Scotts Run Lake; a hike from Hopewell Lake to the historic Hopewell Furnace and back again; and a hike up to and/or around the fire tower on the top of Williams Hill.

Scotts Run Lake

The 21-acre Scotts Run Lake has a lot to offer nature lovers and wildlife watchers. An unmarked trail circles the lake. This probably originated as an access trail for fishermen—the cold-water lake is heavily stocked with trout. But it also provides access to riparian habitat that attracts many different species of birds.

As we circled the lake counterclockwise early one summer morning, we encountered just a few fishermen but many different birds, including **scarlet tanagers,** red-

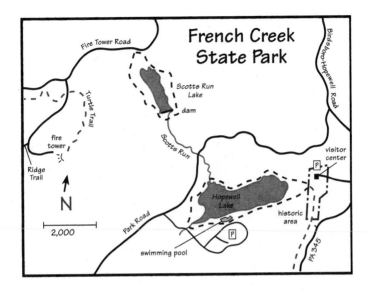

eyed vireos, wood thrushes, and a **veery.** Several mallards in various stages of molt cruised the lake. Molting waterfowl cannot fly and are extremely vulnerable to predators for about 6 weeks while their flight feathers are renewed. They seek safety in numbers, congregating in small flocks like the one we observed.

The trail becomes muddy and difficult at the lake's northwest end. This is where feeder streams trickle into the lake, creating a marshy area. We carefully mucked our way through, walking away from the lake at the wettest spots.

A boardwalk is the best way through an environmentally sensitive, low-lying forest.

Lake to Furnace Loop

Hopewell Lake, the larger of the park's two lakes at 63 acres, was originally dammed by beavers. In the eighteenth century, the owner of the nearby iron furnace built a permanent dam and a raceway to power his waterwheel.

Today, the wooded area between lake and furnace provides an easy, yet rewarding hiking experience. We parked at the swimming pool parking lot (adjacent to the lake) and headed east past the dam to the furnace historic site, a distance of less than 0.25 mile. At this point you are at the south (and farthest) end of the historic site. (A sign requests a small entrance fee to enter the historic site grounds.) From here, we toured the historic grounds on a 0.75-mile trail that leads past various workers' houses, the schoolhouse ruins, a blacksmith shop, the charcoal house, furnace and cast house, barn, and ironmaster's mansion. Most of these buildings can be entered and toured.

The restored "village" of Hopewell Furnace provides a fascinating glimpse at an important period in our nation's history. This furnace and many others in Pennsylvania provided iron for an emerging nation. Since tremendous amounts of charcoal were needed to fuel the large blast furnace, woodcutters timbered the original American chestnut forests of this area and continued to timber subsequent growth for more than 100 years. As you are hiking through the park, look around at the large trees in this mixed hardwood forest and try to imagine when the entire park and beyond was completely clearcut and treeless. As you walk through the furnace site, don't miss the excellent visitor center, where interpretive displays bring to life this slice of American and Pennsylvanian history. (The rest rooms and water fountains are especially inviting for hikers.)

You can make a loop back to the lake on an upper trail that originates behind the furnace and visitor center. The trail forks twice before it crosses the dam and connects with the first trail leading back to the parking lot.

Those who want to make the historic site the focal point of their visit rather than the state park could do this hike in reverse, parking at the Hopewell Furnace parking lot and walking to Hopewell Lake and back.

The Fire Tower

Just west of Scotts Run Lake, at the western edge of the park, stands a fire tower that was a popular destination for years for the scenic vistas it offered. The fire tower itself has been unstaffed and off-limits since 1992, but the area around it is still a popular picnic and hiking destination. There are several ways to explore this area.

Those with small children or physical limitations will want to drive the 0.9 mile up Williams Hill to the fire tower itself, park, and walk the level nature trail at the top. (There are supposed to be maps of this self-guided trail at the now-abandoned ranger station next to the tower, but the box was empty when we visited.) Even before we started walking around this area we saw a scarlet tanager from the parking lot.

Another great hike is along the 0.9-mile access road leading up to the tower. During the spring or fall, or early on a summer morning, this road provides great birding opportunities. And the second half of the hike, when you are most tired, is all downhill!

A third trip we'd suggest is Turtle Trail, a 3.6-mile loop from the parking area at the base of the fire tower access road. This trail leads to the fire tower several different ways. Most direct, and steepest, would be to pick up the trail on the east side of the access road (follow the white blazes). This is about 0.5 mile to the top of the hill. From there you can make the entire loop or cut back down the paved access road. Or you can find the Ridge Trail at the top of Williams Hill (red blazes, northwest of parking area) and cut across to the Turtle Trail (white blazes) on the west side of the access road. The whole thing can be done in reverse, of course, starting from the east side of the access road at the bottom of the hill. Here, as on any hike you take, secure a trail map before you set out.

French Creek State Park contains more than 32 miles of hiking trails, including a self-guided orienteering course. This permanently marked course allows participants to find markers in the woods by using a map and compass. Orienteering enthusiasts call this park the orienteering capital of North America.

Getting There

From the intersection of Rtes. 100 and 23, south of Pottstown, take Rte. 23 west for 7.0 miles, then turn right onto Rte. 345 (heading north) and drive another 0.5 mile to where Rte. 345 veers sharply to the left. Continue on Rte. 345 another 2.0 miles to the park entrance on the left. For a more scenic route through an old, historic part of Berks County, drive west on Rte. 23 for just 3.6 miles to St. Peter's Road. (There's a sign for St. Peter's Village.) Turn right (north) and go 1.5 miles (passing through the village) to a stop sign. Turn left onto Harmonyville Road (SR 4018). Go just 0.2 mile and bear right onto Hopewell Road (SR 4020, later on called Baptism Road). Go 2.2 miles to a stop sign and intersection with Rte. 345. This is the entrance to Hopewell Furnace National Historic Site. Turn left and proceed south on Rte. 345 for a little more than a mile to the sign for the park entrance. Turn right onto Park Road.

The park office is just ahead on the right. Hopewell Lake is just past the office. To get to Scotts Run Lake, continue on Park Road 0.7 mile past Hopewell Lake. Turn left at the lake sign, and drive 0.5 mile to the parking lot and boat launch.

Facilities: The park has 260 year-round camping sites (most with access to showers and flush toilets) and modern furnished cabins. There is also a large swimming pool beside Hopewell Lake, canoe and rowboat rentals, picnic areas, and comfort stations.

Best Time to Visit: Any time spring or fall. Avoid summer weekends, if possible, as this is a heavily visited park.

For More Information: Call the park office at 610-582-9680.

Nearby Attractions: Hopewell Iron Furnace; St. Peter's Village, a restored turn-of-the-century village along French Creek; Marsh Creek State Park, in Chester County; and Daniel Boone Homestead just off Rte. 422 between Pottstown and Reading.

Lancaster County

22. Middle Creek Wildlife Management Area
Lebanon

Hours: Dawn to dusk

If you want to see birds, no matter the time of year, visit Middle Creek Wildlife Management Area. This 6,254-acre public area straddles the Lancaster/Lebanon county line and is managed by the Pennsylvania Game Commission to produce Canada geese. The five thousand Canadas that roam the area testify to the success of the program. Incidental to propagating Canada geese, Middle Creek has become a **prime birding spot** all year long. In fact, Scott rates it as one of the finest birding spots in the country.

For example, visit in mid-February and you will see as many as five thousand **tundra swans** resting on their way north. They assemble on the main 400-acre lake in the off-limits propagation area. Fortunately, the lake borders the main road to the visitor center, so it's easy to just pull over and scan the sea of white. The birds can also be seen from the terminus of Willow Point Trail, a 2,500-foot trek from a parking area just off of Hopeland Road.

Come back two weeks later in early March to catch the peak of the snow goose migration. For no apparent

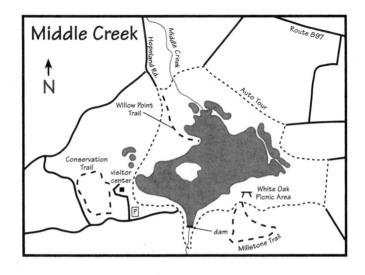

Middle Creek

↑
N

Hopeland Rd.

Middle Creek

Route 897

Willow Point Trail

Auto Tour

Conservation Trail

visitor center

P

White Oak Picnic Area

dam

Millstone Trail

reason, in 1995 northbound snow geese began stopping over at Middle Creek in late February and early March. As many as fifty thousand to eighty thousand **snow geese** stop over to rest and feed as they make their way northward to their Arctic nesting grounds. Throughout the day flocks of several hundred snow geese periodically jump into the air and move from resting areas to feeding grounds. A sky full of these big white birds with black wing tips is a sight to behold as they wheel and glide in formation.

By early May the swans and snow geese are long gone, but families of Canada geese are everywhere. In plowed fields, hay fields, along the roads, and in the ponds, families of four to six goslings follow every adult pair of Canadas. **Bobolinks** and red-winged blackbirds nest in the wet meadows, tree swallows and bluebirds occupy virtually every one of the scores of nest boxes scattered across the area, and migrating songbirds fill the woods.

By summer's end, southward-bound ducks visit Middle Creek to feed and rest. Over the course of the fall, it would not be unusual to see all of the ducks that pass through Pennsylvania stop by at Middle Creek. The waterfowl migration lasts well into December, and a variety of migrating hawks pass through late in the year.

Regardless of when you visit Middle Creek, the first stop should be the visitor center. Catch the orientation film or just spend some time with the excellent collection of mounted birds and mammals that frequent Middle Creek. This is a great way to test your knowledge and learn to identify some of the animals that you've never seen. And don't miss the collection of bird nests and eggs before you leave.

From the visitor center, follow the signs in the parking lot to the Conservation Trail. This 1.4-mile trail begins with a steep but short hill, but we discovered that thereafter the walk is easy. Near trail's end it passes through some low wet spots, so don't be surprised to get your boots wet.

The trail begins where a food plot meets the edge of the woods. The food plot is planted annually in dwarf sunflower, buckwheat, sorghum, and millet. These crops provide food well into winter for a variety of birds and mammals. Along the edge of the woods a swath of trees about 30 feet wide has been cut to provide cover and winter browse. This is a great trail to gain insight into how land managers manipulate vegetation to provide food and cover for wildlife.

At the top of the hill on the edge of the woods, much of Middle Creek is visible. In winter the islands in the large lake are covered with resting geese and swans. In spring many waterfowl nest there.

We headed back along the wooded trail and discovered patch after patch of blooming mayapples and several stands of azaleas. Mayapple flowers are easy to overlook; they hang delicately beneath the plant's deeply cleft, umbrella-like leaves. The pink azalea blossoms, on the other hand, were abundant and set off by long filamentous stamens.

As we continued along the hilltop woodland trail, we came to a regeneration cut. This is a forest management technique where most of the trees have been removed. A few nice tall trees are left behind to seed the area. Den trees and tall dead trees are also left behind to provide cavities for birds and mammals. Because most of the canopy is removed in a regeneration cut, sunlight floods the area, and ground cover flourishes to provide food and cover for deer and other wildlife.

Farther along the trail, we came upon a stand improvement harvest. Here stunted trees and trees of low quality are removed to allow more sunlight to reach the taller, straighter trees. The sunlight also stimulates the growth of ground cover. In an adjacent plot poor-quality trees are marked with red dots to illustrate what a stand improvement harvest area looks like before the trees are removed. This trail turned out to be quite a lesson in forest management.

When we walked the Conservation Trail in May, **the birding was spectacular.** Our list included scarlet tanagers, rose-breasted grosbeaks, indigo buntings, blue-winged warblers, Baltimore orioles, blue-gray gnat-catchers, magnolia warblers, and Canada warblers. We had caught a wave of migrants. Some would surely stay to nest, but the magnolia and Canada warblers would almost certainly move farther north, perhaps to the Poconos.

As we ventured down the trail into a swampy area, the birds and vegetation changed. Skunk cabbage grew alongside the boardwalk, and pin oaks and red maples dominated the woods. Along the way we spotted wood thrushes, ovenbirds, downy woodpeckers, and a black-and-white warbler.

As the trail rose out of the wetland, we journeyed through an old pine plantation. Not too far from here a few years ago, Scott found a patch of pink lady slippers,

Middle Creek visitor center.

a spectacular orchid. Because they are rare and highly prized by collectors (though collecting is prohibited), we will not disclose the orchids' location. Curious botanists will have to search for them.

Near trail's end we crossed a series of footbridges, then came into a meadow by a small pond. On the edge of the pond we noticed several wood duck nest boxes and a variety of elevated platforms for nesting Canada geese. After 2 leisurely hours, we arrived back at the parking lot.

After completing this walk, pick up a self-guided auto tour brochure at the visitor center. When you leave the visitor center, turn left. The first stop gives you a good view of the lake and the large island it surrounds. On our most recent visit, we spotted a rare least bittern skulking among the lakeside vegetation.

A local birder had told us where to look for the bittern. It had been seen for several days running, and its presence had the local birding community abuzz. We pulled our van next to the small pool the bittern had been frequenting and waited. Painted turtles basked in the sun, red-winged blackbirds sang from the cattails, and a swamp sparrow flitted about in some low shrubs. After about 10 minutes Scott started the engine and moved the van forward a short distance. As he did, the bittern flushed from the cattails just 6 feet from the road. The buffy wing patches on this small member of the heron family were obvious as it flew across the pool. Sometimes a vehicle makes a perfect blind.

The second stop on the auto tour is the parking area for the Willow Point Trail. This short (2,500 feet), flat walk should not be missed, especially in February and

March, when swans and snow geese are plentiful. You will see thousands on the main island. In late April and throughout May, this is also a good walk for spotting migrating warblers and other songbirds.

The entire auto tour takes about an hour, depending how long you spend at each of the seven stops. At the fifth stop, the White Oak Picnic Area, you can climb the Millstone Trail for a scenic mountaintop view of the valley below—a round-trip of about an hour. By the end of the tour at the main dam, you will have a much better understanding of how the Game Commission manages a piece of land to produce Canada geese and other wildlife.

Getting There

From Lebanon, take Rte. 897 south about 7.5 miles to Kleinfeltersville. Turn right onto Hopeland Road and proceed about 1.2 miles to the visitor center. From Lancaster, take Rte. 501 north about 16.0 miles to Rte. 897. Turn right onto Rte. 897 and proceed about 1 mile to Kleinfeltersville. Turn right onto Hopeland Road and proceed about 1.2 miles to the visitor center.

Facilities: Restrooms and a drinking fountain are located in the visitor center.

For More Information: Call the visitor center at 717-733-1512. The center is open 8:00 A.M. to 4:00 P.M. Tuesday through Saturday, noon to 5:00 P.M. on Sunday. Closed on Monday.

Nearby Attractions: Watch for horse-drawn buggies and horse-drawn farm equipment in the surrounding Amish countryside.

Easter Bunnies

Easter bunnies symbolize rebirth. Eastern cottontails, the common rabbit found throughout the East, truly are born again—and again, and again, and again. Rabbits multiply rapidly.

Cottontails begin breeding in February unless winter's grip in unusually firm. As delivery time approaches, the female digs a shallow hole in the ground. The nest, about the size of a clenched fist, slants 6 inches inward. The female lines the nest with fur she plucks from her belly and covers the opening with grass, making it difficult to see from above. Nests usually are placed in stands of dense grasses, but sometimes cottontails even sink their nests into well-manicured lawns.

After a 30-day pregnancy, females give birth to four or five blind, naked young. Females nurse their brood only at dawn and dusk. They spend the rest of the day feeding or resting. After about a week in the nest, the young are fully furred and their eyes and ears open. They leave the nest after 14 days. By the age of 1 month the young are weaned and independent.

Meanwhile, mother has been busy. She mates shortly after giving birth, so she's pregnant with a second brood while nursing the first. This is a major reason rabbits are so prolific. A single female might breed four or five times in a year and produce up to thirty-five babies.

Another reason rabbits are so successful is that they have adapted to humans. Cottontails thrive in brushy, man-made habitats—forest edges, fencerows, old fields with scattered brushy thickets.

They spend most of the day resting in a "form"—a well-worn depression on the surface of the ground. It is usually nestled in a clump of dense grass in a thicket or under a brush pile. Occasionally cottontails take refuge in an abandoned groundhog burrow to escape predators or cold, snowy weather. They spend most of their life, however, above ground.

Perhaps the most fascinating aspect of rabbit biology is their diet. Strict vegetarians, cottontails enjoy succulent greens such as dandelion leaves, clover, and grasses as well as the bark of woody species such as raspberry, apple, black cherry, and sumac. In winter, rabbits girdle the stems of shrubs and saplings to eat the nutritious inner bark. This can damage or even kill valuable backyard plantings.

But being vegetarian is hardly unique. What makes rabbits different is they are also coprophagous. That means they eat their own droppings. Rabbits increase the efficiency of their digestive system by recycling the food that passes through their system. They excrete two kinds of droppings. After a meal first moves through the digestive system, rabbits pass soft, green "food" pellets. Rabbits re-ingest these pellets as soon as they are dropped.

During the second trip through the system, vitamins and other nutrients that were not absorbed the first time are assimilated. The familiar piles of round, dark pellets you recognize as rabbit signs are the true end product of rabbit digestion.

Predators, parasites, disease, and foul weather keep rabbit populations in check. Great horned owls, red-tailed hawks, foxes, coyotes, bobcats, weasels, and feral dogs and cats take a heavy toll. Heavy spring rains wash out many nests each year. And each year US hunters kill millions.

The most serious danger rabbits face, however, is habitat loss. Every new mall, parking lot, and subdivision means fewer cottontails. And modern farming methods that require even larger fields to accommodate larger machinery mean fewer fencerows, fewer odd corners, and, ultimately, fewer cottontails.

23. Susquehannock State Park
Holtwood

Hours: 10:00 A.M. to 4:00 P.M.
Monday through Friday

Scenic overlooks almost 400 feet above the Susquehanna River draw people to this beautiful spot in southern Lancaster County. On the half-mile Overlook Trail from the park office to Wissler's Run, an easy, leisurely walk can yield impressive results—wildflowers and warblers in the spring; mountain laurel, rhododendron, and butterflies in summer; migrating birds and brilliant foliage in fall; and bald eagles congregating on the river in winter. **Eagles nest every year** on islands within view of the Hawk Point Overlook. Visitors come armed with binoculars and spotting scopes to watch the majestic birds. The park office even records "eagle updates" on its answering machine when eagle activity is high.

Mt. Johnson Island Bald Eagle Sanctuary is plainly viewable to the south of the overlook. This sanctuary, the first of its kind in the world, has hosted nesting eagles in years past. More recently, however, the eagles seem to prefer other islands nearby.

In addition to the natural wonders are the man-made ones—Peach Bottom Atomic Energy Generating Plant and Muddy Run Hydroelectric Generating Plant, both clearly visible from the overlooks.

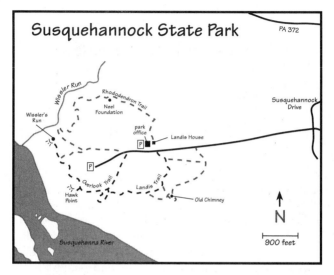

Susquehannock State Park

PA 372

Wissler Run

Rhododendron Trail

Neel Foundation

Wissler's Run

park office

Landis House

Susquehannock Drive

P

P

Overlook Trail

Landis Trail

Hawk Point

Old Chimney

N

900 feet

Susquehanna River

On the blustery March day we visited the park, dozens of turkey vultures soared above the cliffs along the Overlook Trail. Vultures usually migrate south in winter, but these birds hang around the hot water discharges near the power plants, eating dead fish and other carrion. The wind currents that sweep across the Susquehanna and climb the 400-foot-high plateaus on either side provide ideal soaring conditions for vultures.

It's easy to spend several hours bird-watching and botanizing in the overlook areas. But don't miss the treasures waiting in other parts of the 224-acre park. For example, there is a beech tree more than 400 years old and more than 128 feet tall. This ancient beech stands near the foundation of a house occupied by Lieutenant Thomas Neel in the 1800s. It is accessible via the Rhododendron Trail, one of the most beautiful areas of the park as it parallels a stream and meanders through hardwood forest and rhododendron stands. The Landis House is a 150-year-old, two-story stone house adjacent to the park office. Unoccupied and boarded up now, this intriguing structure is the first thing visitors notice when entering the park. We posed beside the house for some photos with Linda's mother, whose maiden name was Landis. Another historic site is Old Chimney, the foundation of an old ironworks located in the southeastern section of the park.

Named for the Susquehannock Indians who originally inhabited the area, the park features 5 miles of interconnecting trails. Hawk Point Overlook, the park's most popular feature, can be reached by Overlook Trail, from a parking lot about 0.1 mile away or by a handicap parking lot even closer. Individual camping sites are not available at this park, but organized group tenting can be arranged.

For more information, call the park office at 717-548-3361 (phones are not monitored full-time) or call Gifford Pinchot State Park at 717-432-5011.

A tree swallow (left) and barn swallow squabble on a fence line.

Getting There

From the junction of Rtes. 272 and 372 at Buck, south of Lancaster, take Rte. 372 west for 2.5 miles. Turn left at the state park sign onto Susquehannock Drive (SR 3009) and drive 2.8 miles to a stop sign. Turn right and continue on Susquehannock Road another 1.3 miles to the park entrance on the right.

Nearby Attractions: Muddy Run Recreation Park, due north of Susquehannock State Park, is owned and operated by the Philadelphia Electric Company (PECO). A 2.7-mile trail encircles a 100-acre lake. The trail is fairly rugged and unlevel, clinging to the edge of the lake's steep, wooded banks. At some spots, it's barely a foot or two from the edge, and as we hiked along, we could just envision youngsters lured too close to the water. You can access the Lakeshore Hiking Trail from the parking lot below the information center. A short interpretive trail is located at the park's north end, and there are several other areas open to hikers but not marked as trails.

But the park's best feature is its information center. It's worth the trip just to experience the interactive displays, learning centers, life-size dioramas, live animals, preserved specimens, bird-viewing area, games and puzzles, energy and environmental exhibits, and much, much more. The center is open 10:00 A.M. to 4:00 P.M. Wednesday through Sunday from April through November, and Tuesday through Saturday from December through March. Admission is free. A park map, with hiking trails marked, is available at the information center. Also, ask about regularly scheduled bird and botany walks.

Bird-watchers flock to the Muddy Run Park and surrounding reservoir areas to observe shorebirds and

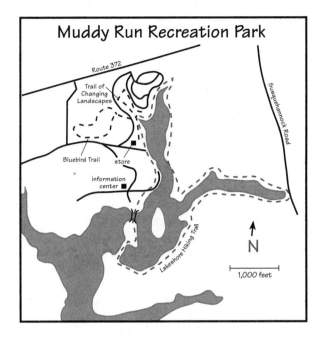

Muddy Run Recreation Park

Route 372

Trail of Changing Landscapes

Susquehannock Road

Bluebird Trail

store

information center ■

Lakeshore Hiking Trail

N

1,000 feet

migrating waterfowl. Ask for birding hot spots at the information center.

For more information, call the park at 717-548-3361.

Getting There

From the intersection of Rtes. 272 and 372, travel 3.6 miles west on Rte. 372, then turn left at the PECO Energy sign for the park. Go another 0.4 mile, then turn left into the park.

New Jersey

24. Rancocas Nature Center
Mount Holly

Hours: 9:00 A.M. to 5:00 P.M. Tuesday through Saturday

Since 1977 the Rancocas Nature Center has served the nature-loving public, courtesy of the New Jersey Audubon Society. This 120-acre tract is part of **New Jersey Audubon's statewide sanctuary system**. Several self-guided trails lead visitors on short treks from the visitor center, a renovated 130-year-old farmhouse, through old fields, wetlands, thickets, pine plantations, and upland woods. A trail guide available at the visitor center will keep you properly oriented.

The trail we recommend is only 0.6 mile long and begins near a large willow oak. Unlike most oaks, which have lobed leaves, willow oak leaves are narrow and have smooth edges. Telltale multiple terminal buds on the tips of each twig, however, indicate that this tree is indeed a member of the oak family.

As the trail continues through an old field, a prickly monster kept reaching out and scratching our bare arms. Multiflora rose was planted widely throughout the East and Midwest back in the 1930s, 1940s, and 1950s. Its aggressive growth habit and sharp thorns made it an ideal "living" fence. And its fleshy hips are great wildlife food.

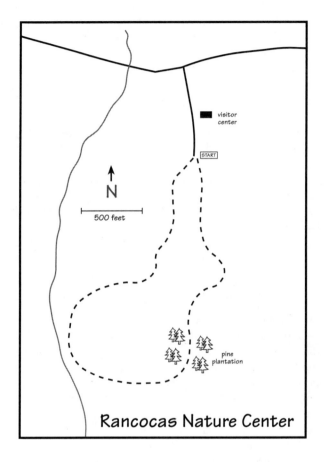

visitor center

START

N

500 feet

pine plantation

Rancocas Nature Center

Unfortunately, this invasive exotic plant is so difficult to control, it has been outlawed in some states. It doesn't seem to realize that "fences" should not invade fields.

To the east, a 183-foot-tall hill is visible. It is the summit of nearby Mount Holly, New Jersey. It is part of a ridge of sand and gravel laid down 100 million years ago when the area was covered by an ancient sea.

When you enter an old pine plantation, you will understand the term monoculture. The canopy is so thick, little sunlight penetrates to the forest floor, so there is virtually no ground cover. As you study the woods, the hand of man is obvious. Nature rarely plants its vegetation in such precise rows.

Three species of conifers can be found in the grove. White pine is native to North America and can be identified by the long soft needles that grow in clusters of five. Austrian pine, on the other hand, has stiffer needles growing in bundles of two. And Norway spruce is characterized by short, stiff, single needles. Study the needles, and you will easily distinguish among these three trees.

When you move from the pine grove into the deciduous woods, look for black locust trees. Thorny branches and leaves consisting of up to twenty small leaflets make them hard to miss. And because it is a member of the legume, or pea, family, the locust bears its seeds in pods. Look for the large seedpods littering the forest floor late in the growing season. Because black locust wood is rot resistant, it was widely planted in Colonial times to provide a renewable source of fence posts.

Depending on the time of year you visit Rancocas, you will see a variety of birds. In winter look for chickadees, titmice, and nuthatches. In spring and summer, you might spy migratory warblers, vireos, and flycatchers. Toward the end of the trail, you will notice some nest

A rogue tree swallow challenges a resident pair for ownership of a nest box.

boxes mounted on poles along the edges of some open areas. Though these boxes are intended for eastern bluebirds, house wrens, chickadees, and tree swallows also use them. From late April through August, these cavity nesters can be seen entering and leaving the nest boxes as they build their nests and feed their broods. Spend some time here and see just how attentive parent birds can be.

Near the end of the trail you will come upon some small trees identified as persimmons in the trail guide. Like hollies, persimmons have separate male and female trees, and only females bear fruit. Resist the urge to taste the fruits. Until the first hard fall frost, persimmons are astringent and absolutely inedible. After a frost, however, sugars form, and persimmons become a favorite food for raccoons, opossums, and humans.

Getting There

From I-295, take the Mount Holly–Willingboro exit (Exit 45A) and go east on Rancocas Road. The center is on the right, 1.8 miles from I-295.

Facilities: Small museum, bookstore, gift shop, reference library, and restrooms.

Best Time to Visit: April through June or for scheduled programs and classes.

For More Information: Rancocas Nature Center, 794 Rancocas Road, Mount Holly, NJ 08060; phone 609-261-2495.

Nearby Attractions: Rancocas State Park is adjacent to the nature center and offers several more miles of hiking trails.

Delaware

25. Brandywine Creek State Park

North Wilmington

Hours: 8:00 A.M. to sunset

The most obvious feature of this excellent park is wide-open space. **Acres and acres of rolling fields** (the park used to be a dairy farm) interspersed with patches of woodland give visitors an **unparalleled sense of freedom.** You have access to all of it and can walk anywhere—even along the top of the old stone fences, an activity that most of us find irresistible.

The 850-acre park was once a dairy farm owned by the du Pont family. Today it encompasses the state's first two nature preserves: Tulip Tree Woods and Freshwater Marsh. Twelve miles of hiking trails join these areas with the rest of the park.

We highly recommend the 0.8-mile Tulip Tree Woods Nature Trail. In fact, this trail alone is worth the trip. The level trail winds through a 24-acre stand of 200-year-old poplar trees interspersed with about ten other species. A pair of giant northern red oaks mark the trailhead, located behind the nature center. From here, the rock-lined dirt trail meanders among massive tulip poplars, red oaks, and beech trees, most over 100 feet high. Walking among the silent giants, we felt as if we

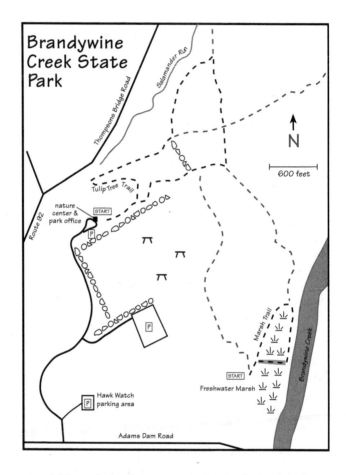

Brandywine Creek State Park

Thompsons Bridge Road

Salamander Run

N

600 feet

Tulip Tree Trail

nature center & park office

START

P

P

Marsh Trail

Brandywine Creek

START

P

Hawk Watch parking area

Freshwater Marsh

Adams Dam Road

Route 92

were visiting a holy place, a natural cathedral—the effect is that awesome. Trail markers and a detailed interpretive brochure enhanced our experience.

We emerged from the trail along a stone wall 200 or

so yards north of the nature center. From there, it was a short hike back to the parking lot and our car.

Marsh Trail was next on our agenda. A series of connecting trails lead from Tulip Tree Woods and the nature center to Freshwater Marsh Nature Preserve. (Get a trail guide at the visitor center.) Or, you can drive your car to the Hawk Watch parking area, south of the visitor center. From the southeast corner of the lot, walk straight down the hill along the stone fence until the fence intersects with a hiking trail. Turn right and walk several hundred yards until you see the blue markers for Marsh Trail.

The half-mile trail encircles the marsh and crosses it at one end on a boardwalk. On a lazy Sunday evening in July we sat on a bench in the middle of the boardwalk and observed yellowthroats, deer, nuthatches, a catbird, a hooded warbler, a downy woodpecker, and a house wren. Most were attracted to Scott's infamous screech owl call. He even got a real screech owl to answer a few times. The dozen or so tiger swallowtails flitting around the nearby buttonbush appeared unperturbed by all the commotion.

The trail continues to the far side of the marsh, right at the edge of Brandywine Creek. We turned left and followed the languid, glasslike creek. Several kayakers flushed a wood duck. We also saw a flicker, pileated woodpecker, and rufous-sided towhee along the water. But we didn't see a bog turtle, nor did we expect to. The Freshwater Marsh is home to the endangered Muhlenberg bog turtle. The turtle is elusive as well as endangered, so hikers are unlikely to encounter one. The bog turtle is small, with orange patches on its head. It is endangered because the draining and filling of marshes throughout its range has severely limited its numbers.

Freshwater Marsh is one of the few locations in Delaware where the bog turtle is found.

Getting There

From the intersection of Rtes. 202 and 92, take Rte. 92 west for 3.0 miles, then turn left onto Adams Dam Road and the park entrance. Or, from the intersection of Rtes. 100 and 141, take Rte. 100 north 2.0 miles to the intersec-

Linda walks on a wall at Brandywine Creek State Park.

Stone fences line the fields at Delaware's Brandywine Creek State Park.

tion with Rte. 92. Turn right onto Adams Dam Road and proceed 0.2 mile to the park entrance.

Facilities: A nature center offers special exhibits and interpretive programs. There's also a gift shop.

Best Time to Visit: Any time. We were surprised how sparsely attended the park was on a Sunday afternoon and evening in late July.

Special Note: Like all Delaware state parks, this one charges a daily fee.

For More Information: Call the park office at 302-577-3534. Call the nature center at 302-655-5740.

PART 2

Overnighters
(more than 100 miles)

Pike County

26. Delaware Water Gap National Recreation Area

Hours: Dawn to dusk at most sites

More than 37 miles of the Delaware River flow through the Delaware Water Gap National Recreation Area, a unit of the National Park Service. An additional 73 miles of river north of the recreation area are part of the Upper Delaware Scenic and Recreational River Area and are open to water recreation. Protected as a Wild and Scenic River, **the Delaware is one of this country's last free-flowing rivers.** Not only does it offer enjoyment and recreation for millions, it provides drinking water for 10 percent of the country's population.

Countless recreational opportunities exist along the river and on the 70,000 acres of public land adjoining it. One of the best, we think, is a hike through wooded ravines along the streams and creeks feeding the river. The area is mountainous, so trails often take you along the **spectacular waterfalls** that abound here.

You could spend an entire summer exploring the Delaware Water Gap and still not see or do everything there is to see and do. The public lands host more than sixty hiking trails. We've described four areas on the Pennsylvania side that we enjoy and that we think will give the nature hiker a good feel for the area. In addition, we list other interesting hiking areas, both in Pennsylvania and New Jersey. (The river forms a boundary between the two states.)

As usual, your first order of business should be to stop at one of the information centers or park offices to secure maps and brochures. Study the information carefully, then plan a visit suited to your time and tastes.

On the Pennsylvania side, Rte. 209, also known as River Road, parallels the river in the recreation area and provides access to the hiking areas we describe. On the New Jersey side, Old Mine Road serves the same purpose, and the Appalachian Trail roughly parallels the river through the recreation area. I-80 crosses through the park's southern tip. The park headquarters is located off Rte. 209, about 9 miles north of Stroudsburg (look for the sign). Call 717-588-2451. Information can also be obtained from the Dingmans Falls Visitor Center (PA), about 7 miles south of Milford (717-828-7802) or the Kittatinny Point Visitor Center (NJ) east of Stroudsburg (908-496-4458).

1. George W. Childs Recreation Site

Three impressive waterfalls along Dingmans Creek draw visitors to the Childs Recreation Site. Hemlocks cover the hillsides surrounding the creek, and sheer rock walls enclose the falls areas. The terrain is rugged, but a 1.8-mile loop hike is easy, thanks to wooden stairs and boardwalks. The trail leads down one side of the mountain and up the other, but at each falls there is a connecting bridge that takes hikers right out over the falls or across the bottom. These bridges increase viewing and photo opportunities. They also allow easy access to both sides of the creek.

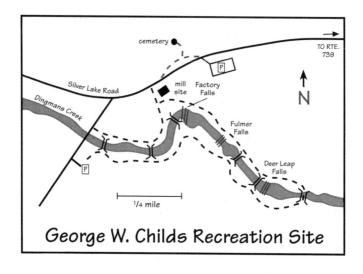

George W. Childs Recreation Site

Near the top of the trail are the ruins of a water-wheel-driven woolen mill, built in 1825 and abandoned 7 years later. A park ranger told us that the mill had once employed eighty people.

Adjacent to the mill site is the top of Factory Falls. This falls, closest to the parking areas, appears to be a popular swimming and picnicking spot. It was quite crowded on the hot August day we visited. Fortunately, there is a direct correlation between crowd size and distance from the parking lot: Less than 0.1 mile downstream we encountered Fulmer Falls, which, in our opinion, is the best of the three. No one was there when we first arrived. The falls is about 70 feet high and has a beautiful, big swimming hole at the bottom. Scott just couldn't resist and jumped in, clothes and all. The water is about 9 feet deep in some spots, and that's in the mid-

Fulmer Falls.

dle of summer, when water levels are low. The falls lie in a natural amphitheater of rocky cliffs surrounded by hemlock forest on top—a truly magnificent setting. A heavy scent of evergreen pervades the area.

Fulmer Falls attracted us not only for its natural beauty but for its name. Linda's maiden name is Fulmer, a relatively uncommon surname. We encountered a historically minded park ranger at Dingmans Falls Visitor Center, who informed us that a John Fulmer established a leather tannery along Dingmans Creek, just upstream from Childs Recreation Site, in 1851. He also established Fulmerville in 1853, which boasted the area's first post office and represented a thriving community. Today it's just a memory.

The trail loops back at the bottom of Deer Leap Falls, another spectacular falls about as high as Fulmer Falls. A bridge crosses at the top of the falls, affording a great view.

The falls loop trail offers some of the best scenery in the Delaware Water Gap. Plan your visit to avoid peak summer crowds. Even then, the trail itself is little used. Most people are primarily interested in swimming.

Getting There

From Rte. 209, about 7 miles south of Milford, take Rte. 739 about 1.1 miles north to Silver Lake Road. Drive another 1.8 miles to a parking area on the left, along Silver Lake Road, or turn left at the access road to another parking area.

Facilities: Picnic tables, comfort station, trash cans, streamside pavilion with benches.

Best Time to Visit: Any time during the spring, fall, or winter. Come here weekdays during the summer, as the area is popular with swimmers on weekends. Area closes at sunset.

Deer Leap Falls.

2. Dingmans Falls Nature Trail

At the Dingmans Falls Visitor Center, a half-mile loop trail along easy terrain leads hikers past two of many magnificent waterfalls along Dingmans Creek.

The first, Silver Thread Falls, is aptly named. **More than 80 feet high,** a thin stream of water falls down a narrow crack in the rock, giving the appearance of a silver thread.

But the water loses its silver appearance and looks reddish brown as it flows in the creek. Tannin from hemlock bark leaches into the stream, giving the water this color. This is the same tannic acid so highly prized by the nineteenth-century leather tanning industry. Eastern hemlock, Pennsylvania's state tree, thrives in the damp, cool, shady environment of the ravine. Its shallow roots allow it to grow on steep slopes, but these same roots leave hemlock vulnerable to drought, erosion, high winds, and heavy snows. These are the reasons you will see many fallen hemlock along the trail to the falls.

A short distance past the falls, the trail crosses a bridge and enters a rhododendron thicket. Rhododendrons grow well in the acidic soil of a hemlock forest. Here the vegetation is so thick it forms a tunnel.

At the far end of the loop you come to a viewing platform facing the 140-foot Dingmans Falls. A trail spur of wooden steps leads to an overlook at the top of the falls. A trail brochure explains that rhododendrons once covered the bare ground leading to the creek, but they were destroyed by people trampling them to get to the creek. The silt that erodes from this bare ground has seriously affected plants and animals using the stream. The area is now fairly well fenced off.

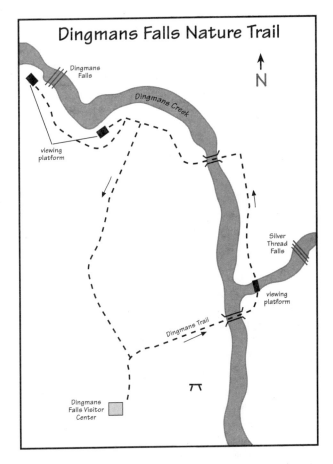

Dingmans Falls Nature Trail

N

Dingmans Falls

Dingmans Creek

viewing platform

Silver Thread Falls

viewing platform

Dingmans Trail

Dingmans Falls Visitor Center

From Dingmans Falls the trail loops back to the visitor center along higher ground.

Be sure to stop at the visitor center while you are there. A video presentation gives visitors an overview of the area. There are interpretive displays, and the park rangers are friendly and knowledgeable. A gift shop carries many different books on the area's natural history and other nature-related topics.

Getting There

From Rte. 209, about 7 miles south of Milford, turn west at the sign for the visitor center and travel 0.5 mile to entrance on right.

Facilities: Visitor center and gift shop, comfort station, water; campground nearby.

Best Time to Visit: Any time. Visitor center is open 9:00 A.M. to 5:00 P.M. daily.

Nearby Attractions: Dingmans Campground, located off Rte. 209 about 1.5 miles southeast of the visitor center and falls, is a private campground operating with a National Park Service permit. It's a full-service campground offering many recreational activities, including swimming in the river. The campground operates from April 15 to October 15. Call 717-828-2266 for information.

3. *Pocono Environmental Education Center*

The Pocono Environmental Education Center (PEEC) is a private, nonprofit facility operating in cooperation with the National Park Service. Located on a 38-acre residential campus, the center extends its activities onto 200,000 acres of adjoining public land. It conducts teacher workshops, school field trips, nature and science education for the general public, organizational retreats, and family vacation programs—all environmentally oriented. PEEC bills itself as "the largest residential center in the Western Hemisphere for environment education."

Twelve miles of hiking trails offer program participants and casual visitors alike the chance to study the natural history of the Poconos. Six trails range in length from 0.25 mile to 5 miles.

Looking for something different, we hiked the Fossil Trail. This 1.5-mile loop trail features **geological history**, but hikers also encounter changing landscapes and biological communities. Markers and a corresponding brochure (available at the main office) help interpret the area. The trailhead is located behind the main building.

The first thing we noticed was a hawk or owl nest in a huge white pine tree. Pines had been lumbered here, as elsewhere throughout the Poconos, but this massive tree was left behind for some reason.

Gray squirrels are everywhere along this trail. We barely walked more than 20 or 30 steps at a time without seeing one, including a black-phase gray squirrel running along an old stone wall. The wall and a nearby stone foundation attest to the farming activities occurring here long ago.

The trail soon leads to a small escarpment, then veers left through a hemlock ravine. After that, we came to a major trail intersection that's a little confusing, but the Fossil Trail (blue blazes) proceeds straight ahead. Shortly thereafter, it forks to the left through a small white pine grove. Next is a steep downhill section covered with slippery loose gravel.

Finally we arrived at the trail's namesake attraction—a bedrock outcrop rich in small marine animal fossils. The center has erected a big sign here illustrating and explaining the three ancient marine animals likely to be found: 1) crinoids, 2) brachiopods, and 3) trilobites. These animals lived 350 million to 400 million years ago, when an extensive part of the country was covered by a shallow ocean.

Hikers are encouraged to hunt for fossils (the outcrop is very steep) but are warned not to take any from this federally owned land. We found that hikers before us had done a lot of work. On two huge tree trunks, dozens and dozens of fossils were lined up for others to view. It was fun poking among them, trying to find good specimens.

After a steep climb back out, we emerged near the center dining hall. A short walk past the dining hall and several cabins took us back to the main building.

Among the other PEEC trails, the Sunrise Trail travels 5 miles over hilly terrain and requires hikers to hold onto ropes while descending from a ledge; the 3-mile Tumbling Water Trail passes by a waterfall; the Scenic Gorge Trail follows a stream for 2 miles through a hemlock ravine; the Two-Ponds Trail (1.5 miles) exposes hikers to the flora and fauna of wetlands and other diverse habitats; the Sensory Trail requires the hiker to be blindfolded while traveling 0.25 mile. Along the way you can compare the feel of different types of bark and leaves, the scents of wildflowers, the sound of birds and insects, and, if you're daring, the taste of various plant materials.

Getting There

From Rte. 209, about 20 miles north of Stroudsburg, turn west at the sign for the Pocono Environmental Education Center. The entrance is about 1 mile from the Rte. 209 turnoff.

Facilities: Forty-five rustic cabins available to PEEC program participants, visitor center, water, and comfort station.

Best Time to Visit: Trails can be hiked any time. Family Vacation Programs and Nature Study Weekends scheduled throughout the year.

For More Information: Call the PEEC at 717-828-2319.

4. Toms Creek Picnic Area

From Toms Creek Picnic Area, hikers can use a wide, graveled trail that follows Toms Creek about 2 miles up a mountain. We only hiked about 0.5 mile upstream because night was falling. In fact, we discovered the trail quite by accident when we stopped at the picnic area to soak hot, tired feet in the stream.

We liked what we saw. The trail was easy and the birding was great (so were the insects at that time of day). Many birds eat insects, so putting up with some buzzing and biting can pay ornithological dividends. A variety of flycatchers, vireos, and warblers often reward the insect-tolerant birder. There are several small dams along the creek built by the Pike County Youth Conservation Corps. We met a park ranger in the parking lot who told us that the trail was beautiful all the way up. We have vowed to return.

Getting There

Located along Rte. 209, about 3.5 miles north of Bushkill.

Facilities: Several picnic tables.

Best Time to Visit: Any time.

Other Notable Spots: Descriptions of these areas come from the National Park Service. Unless indicated, trail lengths are one-way. Distances are approximate, as we found many contradictions between park service figures and other printed sources. Never begin hiking without a trail map. To obtain maps or more information, call the park headquarters at 717-588-2451.

5. Mohican Outdoor Center (New Jersey)

Operated by the Appalachian Mountain Club (AMC), the Mohican Center caters to AMC members and non-members alike. The center is located on Catfish Pond, 9.5 miles north of Kittatinny Point Visitor Center. The Appalachian Trail passes within 0.5 mile of the lodge, as do a number of other shorter trails.

In addition to hiking, center visitors can participate in recreational and educational programs or volunteer to improve area hiking trails. Visitors lodge in small cabins (each with a bathroom and kitchen). The main lodge features a living room/dining room area, kitchen, and bathrooms with showers.

For information on reservation policies and prices or workshop schedules, call the center at 908-362-5670.

6. Mt. Minsi Area (Pennsylvania)

Located near the town of Delaware Water Gap, at the southern end of the national recreation area, Mt. Minsi can be accessed via several trails. From Mountain Road off Rte. 611, the Appalachian Trail climbs about 2 miles to Mt. Minsi, providing excellent views of the Delaware Water Gap. (Park in the Lake Lenape lot.) Just a short

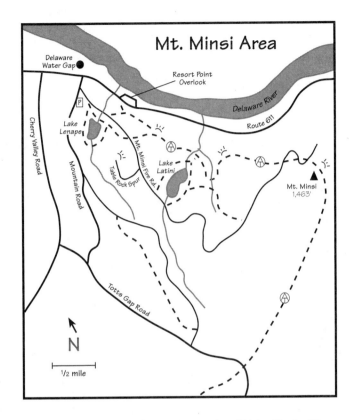

distance beyond Lake Lenape, the Table Rock Spur branches off the Appalachian Trail. Turn right along a gravel road and come to a bare rock terrace, where you'll get another good look at the Delaware Water Gap (0.5 mile to the viewpoint). You can also take the Mt. Minsi Fire Road, in conjunction with the Appalachian Trail, for a 1.5-mile loop hike to Mt. Minsi. From the Resort Point

Overlook parking lot off Rte. 611, cross the highway and follow an old staircase to the top. Turn left to a nearby viewpoint along the Appalachian Trail or right to nearby Lake Lenape, also along the Appalachian Trail.

7. Kittatinny Point Area (New Jersey)

The Kittatinny Point Visitor Center is located across the river from the town of Delaware Water Gap. Most trails in this area are rugged and steep.

The Dunnfield parking area, off nearby I-80, is the starting point for several hikes to the popular destinations of Sunfish Pond and Mt. Tammany. From here, take the Appalachian Trail along Kittatinny Ridge to Sunfish Pond (3.7 miles). The Blue-Blazed Trail branches off the Appalachian Trail to the top of Mt. Tammany (2.5 miles). You can loop back down along the Red Dot Trail (1.5 miles) to the I-80 rest stop area just east of the Dunnfield parking area. Dunnfield Hollow Trail, a former logging road, forks left from the Blue-Blazed Trail and follows Dunnfield Creek (2.5 miles to the Appalachian Trail).

From the Farview parking area along Old Mine Road, follow the Delaware River for 1.5 miles along an old railroad bed on the Karamac Road Trail. The Beulahland Trail also begins here on its steep, 1.5-mile ascent to intersect the Appalachian Trail.

Farther north on Old Mine Road, the Douglas Trail begins its steep, 2.5-mile ascent to the Appalachian Trail and Sunfish Pond from either the Worthington State Forest Office or a parking area 1.0 mile north. (The two trails unite before joining the Appalachian Trail.)

8. Millbrook Area (New Jersey)

Millbrook Village is a re-created late-nineteenth-century rural community located at the intersection of Rte. 602 and Old Mine Road. Visitors can take a self-guided walking tour.

The Appalachian Trail follows the Kittatinny Ridge through this area. An easy 0.5-mile hike to a fire tower and good views can be had by following the trail south from an entry point along Rte. 602 (1.2 miles south of Millbrook Village).

Another 0.5-mile trail with level terrain and wheelchair accessibility follows an old road from Millbrook Village to Watergate picnic area. Wheelchairs can also negotiate the north section of Hamilton Ridge Road Trail, which begins from Old Mine Road, 0.5 mile north of Millbrook.

From the Coppermine parking area between Copper Mine Inn and Pocono Boat Launch, both the Kaiser Road Trail (1.5 miles) and the Coppermine Trail (1.5 miles) join the Appalachian Trail atop Kittatinny Ridge. The Kaiser Trail is a fire road, and the Coppermine Trail passes by historic copper mines.

The Orange Blaze Trail forms a 3.5-mile loop with the Appalachian Trail near Catfish Pond. It can be accessed from Mohican Outdoor Recreation Center off the Camp Mohican Road or from the Appalachian Trail at Rte. 602, 1.2 miles south of Millbrook Village.

For more information on these and other hikes in the Delaware Water Gap National Recreation Area, call the park headquarters at 717-588-2451.

How Acorns Outfox Squirrels

When a red-tailed hawk chases a cottontail, the rabbit hightails it to the nearest thicket. When a large-mouth bass attacks a crayfish, the crayfish darts to the nearest burrow. And when a black rat snake stalks a deer mouse, the mouse relies on vigilance and quickness to elude the snake's deadly coils. These predator/prey interactions are familiar even to armchair naturalists.

But what of plants? Is it possible for plants to escape the jaws of a hungry herbivore? Surprisingly, the answer is yes.

Some plants, such as roses, raspberries, and cacti, arm themselves with thorns. Others, such as milkweeds and locoweed, produce toxic chemicals that poison animals naive enough to eat them. And in the tropics, some species of acacia "permit" ants to live inside their thorns and drink their nectar. In return, the ants attack anything that so much as brushes against their host trees.

But one of the most fascinating botanical antipredator strategies takes place in our own backyards. Acorns are an abundant, widespread, and nutritious food. Every fall squirrels scurry around the forest floor in search of acorns, which they gather and cache in shallow underground middens. At first glance, it seems unlikely that acorns could in any way defend themselves. But they do.

First, we must understand that oaks are classified into two basic groups: the white oaks and the red oaks. Among the differences between the two groups of oaks is the timing of acorn germination.

Red oak acorns, like most temperate plants, lie dormant on the forest floor all winter long and germinate in the spring. Squirrels gather these acorns each fall and store them throughout the woods. In so doing, squirrels act as dispersal agents, ensuring that red oaks get distributed around the forest. They also plant the seeds in suitable fertile soil. Because squirrels never retrieve all their hidden food, forgotten acorns germinate a new generation of red oaks.

Many species of white oaks, on the other hand, germinate soon after they fall to the ground. This adaptation enables white oaks to escape the jaws of squirrels. White oak taproots grow rapidly in the fall and serve as the winter food storage organ. By transferring much of the energy that was in the acorn to the underground taproot, white oaks escape predation by squirrels.

Gray squirrels, however, have learned to beat the white oaks at their own game. Adult gray squirrels can somehow distinguish between red and white oaks (perhaps by smell, taste, or touch). When they find a white oak acorn, they kill it by notching the nut with their sharp incisors and cutting out the embryo. Then the squirrel buries it. A notched acorn is incapable of germinating, but the nut meat remains nutritious until the squirrel retrieves it during the winter.

If this system were perfect, white oaks would be rare. Instead, they are among the most common trees in the eastern deciduous forest. That's because this acorn killing strategy is a learned behavior. It takes time for young squirrels to learn it, so there are always white oak acorns that escape, survive, and germinate. In fact, squirrels notch fewer than half of all the white oak acorns they cache.

Just as animal predators and prey engage in a never-ending battle of attack and counterattack, plants also engage in a continual struggle to survive. Botanical antipredator strategies may be subtle, but they are as effective as any practiced by animals. Note that the operative word is "effective," not "perfect." In nature, perfection isn't required. Adaptive behaviors must work only often enough to ensure that plants and animals achieve life's ultimate goal—successful reproduction.

27. Bruce Lake Natural Area
Promised Land

Hours: Dawn to dusk

Bruce Lake is a **spring-fed, glacier-formed lake**—one of the few publicly accessible natural lakes in the state. But you'll have to work a little bit to see this beautiful spot. Located within the 2,712-acre Bruce Lake Natural Area, the lake can be reached after a more than 2-mile hike. Or, you can ride a trail bike (nonmotorized). Either way, it's a trip worth making.

We began our walk from a trailhead along Rte. 390, entering the mixed forest on a wide, grassy path that appears to be an old road. Ferns carpeted the forest floor. At the first fork, you can bear left and hike just a short distance to the north end of Egypt Meadow Lake, or bear right and continue toward Bruce Lake, skirting the west shore of Egypt Meadow Lake. Egypt Meadow Lake was constructed by the Civilian Conservation Corps in 1935. It's a tranquil, lovely lake, and there are spots where you can get right down to the water to wildlife watch or fish.

We took the right fork for Bruce Lake and hiked about a mile along a trail called the Panther Swamp Trail (it's unmarked at this end). The Bruce Lake Trail forks off to the left just a few hundred yards after the first fork, but this trail is small and overgrown, particularly at the

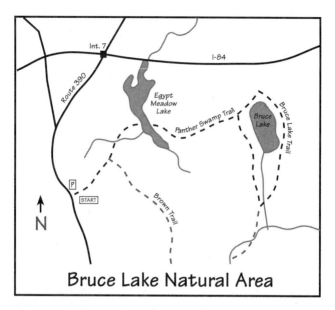

Bruce Lake Natural Area

other end. We continued on the Panther Swamp Trail until it intersected with the Bruce Lake Trail again. Here, turn left and continue.

But first, you may wish to check out the blueberry thickets past a little wooden bridge on the right. On July 30, many of the berries were already ripe, and we picked as many as we could eat. A large flock of robins had the same idea.

We also paused for a rest on the wooden bridge, and Scott did his screech owl call to attract birds. Within minutes he called in a yellow warbler, a catbird, a chickadee, a common yellowthroat, a pewee, and a downy woodpecker. We also admired the mountain laurel and rhododendron thickets all around us.

Proceeding again along the Bruce Lake Trail, we entered a forest study area. Several large trees were ringed with plastic collars, probably for some type of insect research. Soon we came to a wooden bridge crossing the Egypt Meadow Lake. Just before the bridge we sat on a rock at water's edge and observed three Canada geese, a brown creeper, a redstart, wood ducks, swamp sparrows, and lots of red skimmer dragonflies. The arrow leaf was in flower, and we found wild impatiens at the bridge. There's a large, active beaver lodge at the lake's south end.

Bruce Lake is a good mile beyond the wooden bridge. The trail leads through rock-strewn forest. We saw several rocky outcrops and more thickets of mountain laurel and rhododendron. The trail forks again at Bruce Lake, passing around either side of the lake and

The tranquillity of Bruce Lake.

joining again south of the lake. If you continue straight for another 200 yards or so, you'll come to a small, unmarked path on the right that leads right to the water's edge. There's a small, level, grassy clearing with a stone fire ring. It would make a great primitive camp. A giant black oak overhanging the water beckoned to us, and we couldn't resist climbing it. Another 200 yards farther along the trail there is another grassy area along the lake.

On the hike back, we encountered several mountain-bike riders. We assume they were riding a big loop trail from nearby Promised Land State Park. The trail is ideal for mountain biking, and in winter, it's open to cross-country skiers.

We made the trip to Bruce Lake and back in about 3.5 hours, but we'd recommend an all-day hike to truly enjoy the area. Take a picnic and your binoculars. You can even backpack a tent and spend a night or two camping. Primitive camping is allowed throughout the natural area.

Getting There

Delaware State Forest, northeast of Promised Land Lake, Pike County. From the junction of I-84 and Rte. 390, take Rte. 390 south for 0.2 mile to parking area on left.

Facilities: Kiosk with state forest maps at trailhead on Rte. 390.

Best Time to Visit: Any time.

Nearby Attractions: Promised Land State Park, 717-676-3428.

Monroe County

28. Big Pocono State Park
Tannersville

Hours: 8:00 A.M. to sunset

Maintained by the Camelback Ski Association, Big Pocono State Park perches atop Camelback Mountain, high in the Poconos. The park's claim to fame is its access to **spectacular scenic vistas** of eastern Pennsylvania, New Jersey, and New York. Residents of the Philadelphia area commonly flock to the Poconos and to Camelback Ski Area, but few realize the existence of this mountaintop gem.

This 1,306-acre park encompasses the summit and slopes of Camelback Mountain. There are about 10 miles of interconnecting trails up and down the slopes, but we'd recommend a walk on the 1.4-mile paved road that encircles the summit. It's an easy, enjoyable stroll with many opportunities for wildlife watching and scenic vistas.

Park in the summit lot near the office, a stone cabin built in 1908 by Henry Cattell, who originally owned the parklands. According to the park brochure, this office contains a wonderful display of mounted animals, but the office was closed when we visited and no hours were posted. There is also a fire tower on the summit, which has been maintained since 1921 by the Forest Service,

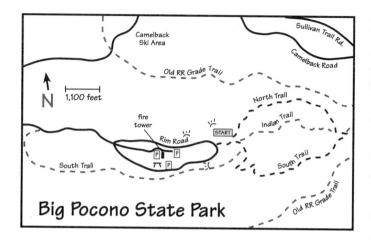

Big Pocono State Park

and a heliport, which has been used since 1963 as a helicopter base for fighting forest fires (both are off-limits to visitors).

Proceeding clockwise around the summit, we first came to an overlook at the top of a Camelback Ski Association chairlift. We enjoyed a magnificent view of the ski resort below.

There are various short spurs that lead from the paved road to a scenic overlook. At one, we sat on a bench and called in a chestnut-sided warbler, a house wren, a chickadee, a catbird, a towhee, and a phoebe. A little farther down the road we encountered a doe and two fawns.

We noticed that the trees and vegetation are cut back along some portions of the road. Obviously, this enhances visibility, and it increases plant species diversity. When trees are cut, sunlight floods the forest floor and triggers an explosion of plant growth. First, herbaceous wildflowers and grasses colonize the opening. Within just a year or two woody shrubs, vines, and saplings invade. This invasion of sun-loving vegetation enhances structural as well as species diversity. Grape and Virginia creeper vines, for example, climb rapidly to avoid the shade of nearby plants and often form twisted tangles. As the vegetation matures, the vertical component of the habitat becomes more complex and the developing forest takes on a layered effect. This provides nesting space for many birds and escape cover for all kinds of wildlife. As a result, these disturbed areas often provide great wildlife viewing. As you stroll by areas that have been cut to improve visibility, be alert for birds,

Virginia creeper is a vine found throughout Pennsylvania.

insects, and other wildlife you haven't seen elsewhere along the walk.

Serious hikers can test their fitness on four interconnected trails passing primarily through the mountain's eastern slopes: North Trail (red blazes), South Trail (yellow), Indian Trail (orange), and Old Railroad Grade Trail (blue). The park staff recommends that inexperienced hikers check on trail conditions and inquire at the park office before hiking the Indian and North Trails. (Both include some steep, rugged terrain.) The South Trail and Old Railroad Grade Trail are both smoother and less steep, and both are also designated as equestrian trails.

All of the trails except the Old Railroad Grade Trail can be accessed from the east end of the summit area. The Old Railroad Grade Trail can be accessed just above Camelback Ski Area, near the bottom of the park road. Don't hike any of these trails without a trail map.

Getting There

From I-80, take Exit 45 at Tannersville and head north on Rte. 715. Make an immediate left at the park sign onto Sullivan Trail. Drive 1.1 miles, then turn left onto Camelback Road at the park sign. This road leads past the Camelback Ski Resort and up to the top of the mountain.

Special Note: Park literature advises motorists not to attempt to pull trailers up Camelback Mountain, as the grade is too steep.

Facilities: The park provides three picnic areas at the summit of Camelback Mountain. There are pit toilets and water at the park office picnic area. Cameltop Restaurant near the summit, operated by Camelback Ski

Area, is readily available to park visitors. Also, the park office is frequently unstaffed, but the nearby restaurant has all-day hours.

Best Time to Visit: Fall, of course, is the time to view spectacular foliage, but this is also the park's busiest time. We visited in late summer and saw no one else there. The vistas would be awesome at any time.

For More Information: There is no telephone access to the park office, but information is available through the Tobyhanna State Park office at 717-894-8336 and 717-894-8337.

Nearby Attractions: The Camelback Ski Resort features many different off-season recreational activities, including an alpine slide and chairlift rides. Nearby state parks include Gouldsboro, Hickory Run, and Tobyhanna. Also nearby is the Delaware Water Gap National Recreation Area.

Luzerne County

29. Ricketts Glen State Park
Red Rock

Hours: 8:00 A.M. to sunset

There is no more magnificent spot in the eastern United States than Ricketts Glen. In the 1930s it was approved as a national park site, but World War II brought those plans to an abrupt halt. The country's loss was Pennsylvania's gain. Since 1942, the state has acquired more than 13,000 acres to protect this precious natural area. The Glens Natural Area became a Registered National Natural Landmark in 1969 and the focal point of the park.

Spectacular waterfalls give Ricketts Glen its superstar status. Two branches of Kitchen Creek cascade through deep wooded gorges, creating more than twenty-two waterfalls. A sign next to each one lists its name and height. The highest is 94-foot Ganoga Falls. The two creek branches eventually meet to flow through Ricketts Glen. Seven miles of hiking trails parallel the streams as they tumble down the mountain.

Many visitors enjoy hiking down one branch of the creek to "Waters Meet" and back up along the other—a total distance of about 3 miles. That's what we did when we first discovered Ricketts Glen in the early 1970s. We walked from falls to falls, sitting at each to absorb the

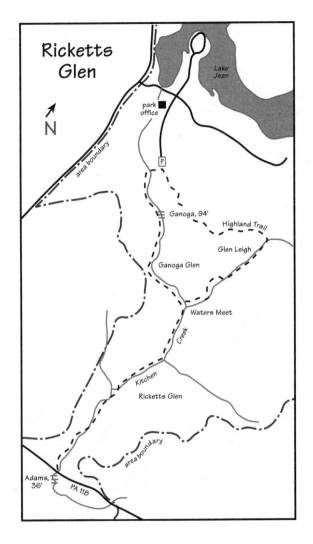

Ganoga Falls—Ricketts Glen State Park.

sights, sounds, and smells of an ancient forest. We learned to hit the trails early and stay late.

More recently we shared our favorite park with our daughters, Nora and Emma. They were as enthralled as we were with the area's grandeur. And just as we did more than 20 years ago, they kept pretending they were the first humans ever to set foot beside the magnificent falls and ancient trees. What must those lucky individuals have thought of this place!

The wooded trails cut through stands of giant pines, oaks, and hemlocks, many towering over 100 feet high, with diameters up to 5 feet. Park literature reports that many of these trees have been standing more than five hundred years. Ring counts on some fallen trees reveal ages of up to nine hundred years. We get the distinct impression of being in a holy area when we stand amidst these silent giants.

On our hike with the girls, we tried something different. Instead of hiking down Ganoga Glen to "Waters Meet" and then back up through Glen Leigh, taking the Highland Trail at the top back to the parking lot (by far the most popular route), we decided that it would be easier on the girls if they could just hike straight down the mountain to the bottom. When we reached "Waters Meet," which is roughly the halfway mark, Scott hiked back up to the parking lot to get the car, while the girls and Linda finished descending the mountain.

There are only three falls below "Waters Meet," and those are smaller than most of the other falls, but they are still spectacular. On a hot July afternoon we just couldn't resist soaking our hot, tired feet in the clear, cold water. Perched on a streamside rock, our feet dangling in the creek, it was difficult to imagine a better place in the world.

Perhaps it was that relaxing soak that dulled our senses. At any rate, we missed a critical fork in the trail. About a mile or so from our destination, we bore right at an unmarked fork when we should have gone left. Linda thought that the right fork looked much more official than the left, which appeared to be a narrow spur leading down to the water.

The "wrong" trail soon became a muddy "road" through mature woods. We realized after awhile that we had probably come the wrong way, but because we weren't sure, we continued, reasoning that at least we were heading in the right general direction. And then there was the compelling birdsong we kept hearing just ahead—a loud, melodic series of trills that lasted about 7 seconds. Linda and the girls had never heard anything like it, and it just added to the enchanted, almost surreal atmosphere of the woods at this point. We kept trying to catch a glimpse of the bird, but we never did. Later, upon hearing a description of the song, Scott recognized it immediately as that of a winter wren. He had first seen and heard the bird in Maine, and he knew of its exceptionally long song (5 to 7 seconds). Despite its beautiful, almost hypnotic song, the winter wren is small and drab brown, with a short, stubby tail. Its song appears to be its only distinguishing characteristic.

After what seemed like a long, anxious time of wondering where exactly we were going (and, yes, we had the map, but it didn't show that trail we had taken), we finally heard voices below us and realized that there was another trail just east of us (the right one!), at the bottom of the ridge we were walking. Soon we came to a ranger station and inquired about our whereabouts from the ranger on duty. He informed us that we had worked our way along an upland trail and had emerged only several hundred yards west of the parking lot on PA 118—our original destination.

The highway crosses Kitchen Creek at this point, and the last falls on state park property—the 36-foot Adams Falls—can be viewed from the bridge on the south side of the highway. Even if you don't have the time or inclination to hike to any other falls, take the time to view this one. It's the only one you can drive right to.

When hiking the falls area, you have several options. One is to park in the lot at the top of the mountain (just south of the park office) and hike down to "Waters Meet" and back up again. Another is to park at the top, hike about 3 miles straight down the mountain to the parking lot on PA 118, and have someone pick you up there. Or, you could park at the bottom of the mountain and hike either halfway up, to "Waters Meet" and back, or all the way to the top along one branch of the creek and down along the other. You could do this last option in reverse, of course, but don't forget you'd be ending your hike with a 3-mile trudge up a steep mountain.

Several words of caution are in order here. First, the trails are steep and narrow in many places and extremely slippery when wet. In some places, you'll be stepping over big rocks and fallen tree trunks. **This is *not* a hike for those who are feeble or faint of heart.**

Although Ricketts Glen is the heart and soul of this park and the major attraction, the park features several other trails—20 miles' worth in all. One of the more interesting and remote is the Mountain Springs Trail leading to (or from, depending upon where you start) the 40-acre Mountain Springs Lake on adjacent Pennsylvania Fish Commission land. The lake is about 2 miles from the family cabins area or 3 miles from the parking area at the top of the Glens Natural Area.

The other attraction at Ricketts Glen State Park is Lake Jean. At 245 acres, this lake offers exciting opportunities for canoeing, rowboating, and sailing. There is also a guarded swimming beach.

Getting There

From I-80 in Bloomsburg, take Exit 35 and head north on Rte. 487 for about 30 miles. This road leads directly to the park. However, the last 4 miles of this route are extremely steep and should be avoided if you are pulling a heavy trailer. Instead, approach the park on Rte. 487 heading south from Dushore.

Facilities: The park offers 120 campsites and 10 modern cabins open year-round. There's also a swimming beach and boat rental concession at the east end of Lake Jean. Picnic areas and comfort stations abound.

Best Time to Visit: Ricketts Glen is breathtakingly beautiful any time of year. In spring, there is no better place to see nature rejuvenate itself. In summer, it's a cool lush haven. In the fall, the colorful trees steal the limelight from the falls. And in winter, there is no more magical place than a snow-covered and frozen Ricketts Glen. This is a popular park, however, so we'd suggest you avoid the area on summer weekends.

For More Information: Call the park office at 717-477-5675.

New Jersey

30. Edwin B. Forsythe National Wildlife Refuge
Oceanville

Hours: Daily, sunrise to sunset

Named in honor of the late conservation-minded congressman from New Jersey, the Edwin B. Forsythe National Wildlife Refuge was created in 1984 by combining two existing refuges. The Brigantine and Barnegat Refuges date back to 1939 and 1967, respectively. Today the consolidated refuge protects more than 39,000 acres of **critical coastal habitat.**

The primary purpose of the refuge is to ensure the survival of tidal wetland and shallow bay habitat for use by migratory birds. Every year hundreds of thousands of **ducks, geese, wading birds, and shorebirds** use the refuge. Spring and fall are the best times to visit. That's when huge numbers of migratory waterfowl move up and down the Atlantic coast. Summer visitors will find wood ducks, mallards, black ducks, Canada geese, herons, egrets, rails, and ospreys, while a winter visit will find large numbers of black ducks, brant (a type of goose), snow and Canada geese, tundra swans, and a variety of raptors. In fact, in winter the Forsythe Refuge is one of the East Coast's best places to observe

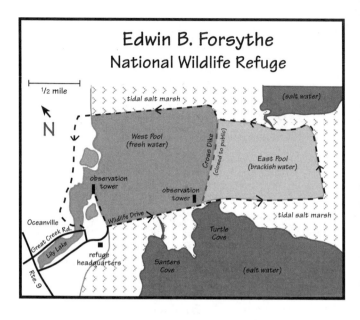

½ mile

N

tidal salt marsh

(salt water)

West Pool
(fresh water)

Cross Dike
(closed to public)

East Pool
(brackish water)

observation
tower

observation
tower

tidal salt marsh

Oceanville

Wildlife Drive

Great Creek Rd.

Turtle
Cove

Lily Lake

Rte. 9

refuge
headquarters

Santers
Cove

(salt water)

waterfowl, marsh hawks (harriers), rough-legged hawks, and bald eagles.

We will emphasize the Brigantine Division of the refuge because it is much more accessible than the Barnegat Division farther north. After parking near the Brigantine headquarters, hikers have two options. The Acre's Woodland Trail is a short 0.25-mile ramble through some upland woods. In May and June the trees are filled with warblers, vireos, and other migratory songbirds. Just beyond headquarters, before you enter the one-way auto drive, Leed's Echo Trail explores the salt marsh. This 0.25-mile boardwalk tour is a great introduction to salt marsh life. Most visitors to the Jersey shore know only the pristine sandy beaches that line the popular tourist towns. In contrast, stinky, mucky salt marshes teem with life. Unfortunately, biting insects are part of the bargain, so wear long sleeves and pants and bring insect repellent when the weather's warm.

Unlike most of the places featured in this book, where the emphasis is on nature walks, Brigantine's primary attraction is an 8.0-mile self-guided Wildlife Drive. Pick up a brochure at headquarters, and plan to spend at least an hour making the one-way loop. If you enjoy seeing large numbers of birds, plan to spend the entire morning. If you're really ambitious, you might try to hike or bike the entire 8.0-mile loop. We'd suggest a bike ride because there's little shade on the loop, and a walk might take 3 or 4 hours. Because waterfowl are so abundant here, the loop ride also makes a great wildlife watching experience for disabled nature lovers.

The drive begins with a short two-way spur to an observation tower. Kids enjoy climbing the tower, and the panoramic view from the top is impressive. The contrast between the wild, undeveloped marsh and the glitz of Atlantic City in the background is thought provoking.

As you begin the one-way tour, you are driving on the South Dike, an old railroad bed that once connected Brigantine Island to the mainland. It now serves as the southern edge of a dike system that contains two large pools of water. The West Pool contains fresh water, the East Pool is brackish (a mixture of fresh and salt water). As you begin the drive, the West Pool is on your left and the salt marsh is on your right.

Fresh water is a critical element of any well-balanced salt marsh. The 900-acre West Pool is specifically managed to attract migratory waterfowl. Though many ducks and geese spend time in brackish water, they flock to fresh water to drink and bathe. Fresh water is particularly important for washing salt residues from feathers.

Depending on the time of year you visit the refuge, pond water levels will vary. By manipulating water levels, refuge managers stimulate the growth of aquatic and semiaquatic vegetation. These plants produce the foods that attract huge numbers of migratory waterfowl.

In contrast to the West and East Pools, the tidal waters of the salt marsh to your right ebb and flow twice each day. In Turtle Cove low tides expose mud-flats teeming with small invertebrates that attract shore-birds by the thousands. In May and June horseshoe crabs spawn on these flats, and shorebirds feast on the freshly laid eggs.

Opposite Turtle Cove, another observation tower rises above the salt marsh. Scan the area for flocks of waterfowl. In November and December white oceans of snow geese cover some areas, while huge dark flocks of brant and black ducks assemble in others.

As you continue past the tower, the East Pool is now to your left. This 700-acre shallow impoundment is carefully managed to maintain its brackish character. This mixture of fresh and salt water supports a rich diversity of invertebrates, which are important food for many shorebirds. From July through September, the mudflats and shores of the East Pool attract most of the plovers and sandpipers that pass through the area.

Scattered throughout the East Pool, you can see a number of small islands. These islands provide relative-

*A Canada goose hides behind the vegetation at Forsythe
National Wildlife Refuge.*

ly safe nesting and brood-rearing habitat for geese, black ducks, gadwalls, and mallards. Look for goslings to appear in May and ducklings in mid-June.

Occasionally you may see blackened burn areas. Refuge managers periodically burn off large accumulations of plant material to rejuvenate the soil and stimulate native plant growth. In spring new growth quickly turns burned areas a lush verdant green. Controlled burns eliminate the buildup of flammable plant debris. Refuge staff hope this will prevent a repeat of a 1965 wildfire that destroyed most of the vegetation on the refuge.

Keen observers may notice deep ditches scattered throughout the shallow East and West Pools. These zones of deeper water provide habitat for fish, which in turn provide food for larger wading birds such as great blue herons and great egrets. The ditches also promote water circulation throughout the pools. This increases the oxygen levels in the water and helps reduce summer water temperatures.

The final leg of the drive takes you through an upland area of fields and forests. Refuge staff mow the fields regularly to keep plant succession at bay. Otherwise, the fields would revert to woodlands. Watch for deer, rabbits, squirrels, and songbirds along this part of the route.

Getting There

Take the Atlantic City Expressway east to Rte. 9 north. Proceed north on Rte. 9 to Oceanville. Turn right onto Great Creek Road and follow signs about 1 mile to refuge.

Facilities: Information office and auditorium at refuge headquarters are open weekdays, 8:00 A.M. to 4:00 P.M.

Best Time to Visit: Spring and fall.

Special Note: A modest fee is charged to enter the refuge. Biting insects can be ferocious from mid-May through September. Come prepared with long sleeves, long pants, and insect repellent.

For More Information: Contact the Refuge Manager, Edwin B. Forsythe National Wildlife Refuge, Great Creek Road, P.O. Box 72, Oceanville, NJ 08231, or call 609-652-1665.

Nearby Attractions: Atlantic City is just south of the refuge.

31. The Wetlands Institute
Stone Harbor

Hours: 9:30 to 4:30 Monday through Saturday, 10:00 to 4:00 Sunday (closed Sunday and Monday October 15 through May 15).
Admission: $4, children $2

Explore the intertidal salt marshes of New Jersey's southern shore region at the Wetlands Institute. We loved this up-close and personal view of the coastal wetlands, and so did our daughters. The institute is a non-profit research and public education facility **dedicated to preservation of coastal wetlands.** Six thousand acres of public wetlands surround the complex. Visitors can enjoy interactive exhibits, wildlife art, aquariums, microscopes and spotting scopes, and special programs.

The highlight, though, is the salt marsh trail. The trail begins along the east side of the education building. (Pick up a trail guide at the trailhead. It's a detailed and informative booklet.) Just as we were about to begin the trail, our girls noticed narrow, winding stairs leading to an observation deck. They headed right up and we followed. The observation deck gave us a bird's-eye view of the salt marsh and the entire trail area. Even more exciting was the osprey nesting platform directly ahead. With our binoculars we got a great look at two adult ospreys perching on the platform.

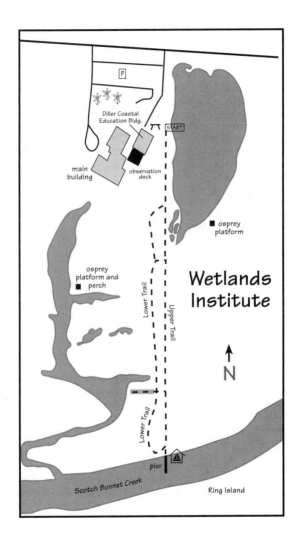

Less than a mile in length round-trip, the trail features numerous natural wonders. There are thirteen marked and numbered sites highlighting some aspect of ecology or plant and animal life—for example, the exposed mudflats, home to fiddler crabs and mud snails and the wading birds that feed on them. Each marked station corresponds to a detailed explanation in the trail guide. **Salt marshes**, characterized by vast, grassy meadows, are among the most productive ecosystems in the world. And that fact hits home when you observe the abundant plant and animal life along the trail. It's not unreasonable to expect to see thirty bird species on a good day. On our visit in August, we observed a variety of gulls, terns, egrets, herons, and an osprey.

The trail proceeds from the education building (the northeast side of the complex) to Scotch Bonnet Creek and loops back again.

One side of the trail loop goes "upland" on a hard-packed surface that leads to a 100-foot pier overlooking the tidal creek. Bayberry, winged sumac, autumn olive, and red cedar are among the most prolific trees and shrubs in this sandy area.

Bayberry has leathery evergreen leaves, and in late summer bears a crop of waxy fruits that attract fruit-eating birds, such as thrushes, waxwings, grouse, and quail. Autumn olive is a dense thorny shrub characterized by silvery underleaves and red fleshy fruits. Red cedar is conspicuous because it has both scaly "leaves" and sharp spiny needles.

The other side of the trail is marshy. Here, the trail becomes spongy and wet, characterized by black mud and the smell of rotten eggs (decomposing plants and animals). *Spartina* grasses dominate the marsh, because they can thrive in the changing tides and salty mud. A boardwalk leads walkers right to the edge of a small creek. From the boardwalk at high tide, it's possible to see grass shrimp and minnows feeding among the grasses. During low tide, the boardwalk passes through mudflats. This is when you're likely to see waders feeding on crabs and snails.

During each season, the trail offers a unique show of flora and fauna. In spring, diamondback terrapins (a type of turtle) come up out of the creeks to dig nests and lay their eggs on high ground. If you see a small, circular hole along the upland trail, you can assume that it's an abandoned terrapin nest. The trail guide cautions walkers to watch for tiny diamondback terrapins emerging to head for open water. (Those hatched in June emerge in August; those hatched late in summer will winter underground and emerge in the spring.) So it's

Laughing gulls are abundant along the beaches at the Jersey shore.

possible to see the tiny creatures, barely more than an inch long, through much of the spring and summer. We looked carefully but didn't notice any.

Early summer is the time that laughing gulls nest on Ring Island (visible from the pier). Later in the summer, migrating tree swallows feed on bayberries along the upper trail.

Bird (raptors and warblers) and butterfly (monarchs) migrations highlight the fall season.

Even in winter, the salt marsh teems with life. Northern harriers (marsh hawks) fly low over the marsh grasses in search of rodents. Brant and black ducks, mergansers, and buffleheads spend the winter, as do the great blue herons.

Some advice: Wear appropriate footwear, because the trail can become quite wet and muddy out in the salt marshes. Also, the flying/biting insects are terrible during the warm months, so wear long pants and a long-sleeved shirt, and use insect repellent.

Getting There

From the Garden State Parkway, take Exit 10 and proceed east on Rte. 657 (Stone Harbor Boulevard) for about 2 miles to the Wetlands Institute on the south (right) side of the road. A sign clearly marks the entrance.

Nearby Attractions: Bellplain State Forest. Town of Stone Harbor, built on a barrier island that shelters the salt marshes.

For More Information: Call the institute at 609-368-1211.

The Shore

The summers of the early 1960s linger fondly in my mind. My family vacationed at the south Jersey shore where an aunt and uncle rented a house each year. My time there was pure fun—days at the beach, nights on the boardwalk.

But the appeal of those attractions faded as I grew older. I began to spend more time roaming the beach and studying its inhabitants. Occasionally I'd save enough money to rent a boat to explore the salt marshes.

I came to see the shore as a special and very different place. Even now, on those rare occasions I get to the beach, I walk the surf and introduce my daughters to beach creatures. Most are common, but to an inlander like me, they hold an intense and enduring fascination.

Next time you head to the beach, try relaxing by getting to know the shore's wild side. Begin by looking at the physical environment from a different perspective.

Take the wind, for example. It shapes the seashore, even on still days. Ocean winds that may originate thousands of miles away propel the waves that beat rhythmically and incessantly upon the beach. To live in the surf zone, creatures must either anchor themselves to the bottom, swim strongly, or float aimlessly.

Another physical feature that dominates every seascape is the tide. Powered largely by the gravitational pull of the moon, tides peak and ebb twice each day. But the rhythm of the tides is not constant from day to day. In fact, the schedule advances 50 minutes each day, due to the rate at which the moon orbits the earth. Yet as surely as the sun rises each morning and waves pound the beach, so, too, do the tides rise and fall.

Within this dynamic world of winds, waves, and tides live myriad species of wondrously adapted plants and animals. Some, such as gulls and horseflies, are obvious and often annoying. But most are inconspicuous and must be searched out.

Visit the beach at sunrise. You'll beat the crowds, and the beach's slate will be washed clean. In May ferocious-looking horseshoe crabs invade the shoreline to lay eggs. These harmless crustaceans have roamed the seashores for millions of years. Their continued presence is nature's version of continuity.

Watch for small egg-shaped critters that seem to vanish from the sand without a trace. They are mole crabs, ghostly creatures that appear and disappear in the blink of an eye. I've found these often while building sand castles.

Speaking of apparitions, if you get to the beach before dawn, you may glimpse a ghost crab dart across the sand. Colored to match the sand they live on, ghost crabs blend into the beach when they stop moving.

And no description of the eastern shore would be official without mention of jellyfish and clams.

Nothing can ruin a day on the beach faster than an influx of jellyfish from a storm the night before. Their stinging tentacles cause an itchy rash that may last for several hours. In open water these stinging tentacles paralyze fish and other prey that wander within their reach.

To find live clams, on the other hand, just dig beneath the small holes that dot the sand at the water's edge. The holes are the tips of siphon tubes through which flows the oxygen- and food-rich water that sustains the clams. With any luck, you'll find such wonderfully named species as quahogs, coquinas, razors, and jackknives.

And if you've been living right, you may glance out at the horizon and see a school of dolphins frolicking just offshore. It's a sight you'll long remember.

If a seaside nature walk sounds like fun, pick up a copy of the Audubon Society nature guide entitled *Atlantic and Gulf Coasts* or AMC Books' *Seashells in My Pocket,* and let it be your guide.

32. Cape May

Hours: Dawn to dusk

We got to the beach just before dawn. Already, laughing gulls and common terns patrolled the surf zone, ever watchful for small crabs stranded by a surging wave. Laughing gulls are easy to recognize; they have black heads and, appropriately, voices best described as a laugh. Common terns are trimmer, with black caps, a black-tipped red bill, and a forked tail.

We decided to sit for 30 minutes, armed only with binoculars and Peterson's *Field Guide to the Birds.* We were hoping for a glimpse of two endangered species known to nest in the area—piping plovers and least terns.

Offshore, high above the waves, an osprey flew back and forth along the coast. Its deeply bent wings made it easy to identify, even in silhouette. Just above the water a line of five brown pelicans flew southward. Far off-shore, a raft of gulls too distant to recognize bobbed up and down on the rolling waves.

A glance at the dunes brought good views of singing yellow warblers, displaying male red-winged blackbirds and territorial song sparrows. Even if we had not been able to see the rusty streaks on the yellow warbler's breast, its song was diagnostic—"Sweet, sweet, sweet, I'm so sweet!" The red-wing's ebony body contrasted vividly with its bright red epaulets. Even the drab song

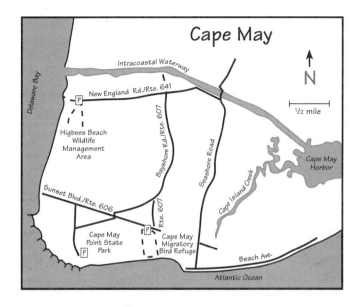

sparrow has a distinctive feature: its streaky breast
markings converge to form a dark central spot.

Just before our self-imposed deadline expired, Linda
noticed movement on the beach in front of the dunes. A
quick check with our binoculars confirmed our suspi-
cion—a piping plover. The bird's narrow, dark breast
band caught Linda's eye. Otherwise this small sandy-
colored shorebird is tough to spot on the beach.

As we watched the plover through our binoculars,
another bird flew through the field of view. Gray above,
white below, black cap and black-tipped yellow bill—we
suspected it was a least tern. The bird landed about 50
yards away, and we got a better look. When it took off,

we noticed its long narrow wings and forked tail. Definitely a least tern, the smallest tern in North America. Two endangered species in five minutes was a new record for us.

As we followed the trail across a wet meadow back to the parking area, a loud bubbly sound floated across the grasses. The bobolink's flight song is one of Scott's favorites. When it perched on a reed, we could see the white rump and shoulders and buffy hind neck that distinguish this member of the blackbird family.

Those are just some of the birds we saw on a June morning at the **Cape May Migratory Bird Refuge.** The walk from the parking lot on Cape May's Sunset Boulevard to the beach and back is less than a mile, but it is always a fascinating journey. In the spring, migratory

Migrating shorebirds gather at south Jersey beaches in May to feast on horseshoe crab eggs.

songbirds feed and rest in the meadows on their way north. During the summer, shorebirds, gulls, and terns are everywhere. In the fall, hawks, songbirds, monarch butterflies, and migratory dragonflies head south through the area. And in the winter, loons, gannets, and sea ducks can be seen offshore.

Welcome to Cape May, one of the **finest bird-watching spots in North America.** To birds migrating north in the spring, Cape May is the southernmost spit of land across the Delaware Bay. To southbound birds in the fall, it's where birds are funneled to await weather conditions that are favorable to cross the bay.

Because Cape May is such a bird-friendly place, each May it hosts the "World Series of Birding." Teams from all over the world converge on south Jersey to see who can see the most species of birds in a 24-hour period. The winning count often tops two hundred species.

The Cape May Migratory Bird Refuge is just one of several prime birding areas in south Jersey. If you are new to birding, call the Cape May Bird Observatory (609-884-2736), and ask when the next bird walk is scheduled. There is usually one regularly scheduled bird walk each week.

If you're lucky, you might even get to bird with Pete Dunne. Pete is the observatory's director and one of the finest birders in the world. He's always eager to help new birders enjoy the show. A morning with Pete is worth a month of Sundays studying books and recordings. And he is generous with his quick wit. His description of birding to a group one Tuesday morning, for example, was right on target: "Birding is a lot like going to an art gallery, except the paintings hide."

The second stop on the Cape May tour is **Cape May Point State Park**. Continue west on Sunset Boulevard about a mile and follow the signs. A picturesque 157-foot-tall lighthouse marks the spot. Its 350,000 candle-power beam can be seen 19 miles out to sea.

The 190 acres of the park was used as a coastal defense base during World War II. Though the bunker was originally positioned 900 feet from the ocean, severe coastal erosion has washed away most of the sand between the bunker and the sea. At low tide, gun mounts can be seen in front of the bunker.

From the parking lot, you can see a large hawk-watching platform and a covered observation area to watch seabirds. Mingle with the regulars, and you'll probably be invited to see some distant bird through their spotting scopes.

When you are ready to walk, start on the 0.5-mile self-guided Red Trail. This trail is wheelchair accessible, so it's a great place for disabled naturalists. Be sure to pick up a trail guide at the office before you begin. It will help you understand the plants and animals that inhabit the area.

One of the most conspicuous plants of coastal dunes is bayberry, a dense shrub with dark green deciduous leaves. In the fall its waxy berries are the preferred food of yellow-rumped warblers (call 'em "butterbutts" to impress your birding friends) and tree swallows. A similar plant, wax myrtle, also produces a fall crop of waxy berries, but wax myrtle is evergreen and grows as a small tree.

As you proceed along the Red Trail, you will encounter another conspicuous evergreen. Pitch pine is a

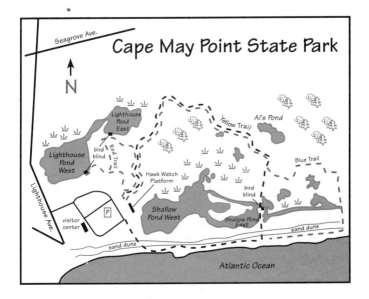

dominant tree in both the New Jersey Pine Barrens and throughout the Cape May area. Its bark is thick and platelike, and its needles are grouped in clusters of three. You will even notice groups of needles arising directly from the main tree trunk.

Among the highlights of this short walk are two blinds that overlook the East and West Lighthouse Ponds. These rain-fed, freshwater ponds attract a variety of marsh birds and larger mammals. Approach and enter the blinds quietly, and you might spot rails, bitterns, green herons, muskrats, or a fox. If you have a telephoto lens for your camera, you might even get some good wildlife shots.

The tall reed grass that dominates much of the marsh is *Phragmites,* an Old World import. Typically it drives out native cattails and overruns disturbed wetlands. Muskrats, marsh wrens, and red-winged blackbirds thrive in *Phragmites* marshes, but it is otherwise poorly regarded for its value to wildlife.

If you find the Red Trail too short, try the Yellow (1.3 miles) or Blue (3.0 miles). Both take you through a combination of woods and marsh, and both conclude with a nice stroll along the sandy beach.

Before you leave Cape May Point State Park, be sure to stop by the visitor center. Displays explaining the region's natural and cultural history answer many of the questions that come to mind while hiking the area. Saltwater tanks display samples of common marine life, and

Linda and the girls explore a Cape May beach.

during the spring and summer fresh-picked wildflowers are arranged and identified. One of the more popular exhibits explains the origins of "Cape May diamonds," clear quartz crystals made smooth by the action of sand and surf.

Among the best places to search for Cape May diamonds is the beach at the end of Sunset Boulevard. You'll know you're at the right place when you see the sunken concrete ship just offshore. Stroll the white sandy beach and keep your eyes peeled for small glistening objects. And keep your binoculars handy. A variety of shorebirds frequent New Jersey's southern tip, and gulls and terns are constant companions.

Our third recommendation for the immediate Cape May vicinity is **Higbees Beach Wildlife Management Area.** From the Cape May Migratory Bird Refuge, cross Sunset Boulevard (Rte. 606) and travel north on Rte. 607 about 2 miles to Rte. 641. Turn left and park where the road ends. Several trails radiate from this parking area. One leads directly to the beach. This area consists mostly of woods and fields and is best for songbirds in May and June.

One of the world's **truly spectacular natural phenomena** is the congregation of hundreds of thousands of shorebirds along the beaches of the Delaware Bay in May. As shorebirds migrate to Arctic nesting areas, they stop to feast on the eggs of horseshoe crabs, which spawn on beaches at this time. Countless horseshoe crabs, primitive crustaceans named for their distinctive shape, drag themselves ashore to lay their eggs in the sand. A variety of shorebirds, but red knots and ruddy turnstones in particular, feast on the caviar. For two

Cape May sunset.

weeks they stay, gorging themselves and as much as doubling their body weight. Then it's off to nest on Arctic breeding grounds. Thousands of gulls also descend on these beaches to eat the vulnerable crabs as they haul themselves into shallow water to lay their eggs.

This spectacle can be seen along many Delaware Bay beaches, but one convenient to Cape May is **Reed's Beach.** Travel north on Rte. 47 about 14 miles from Cape May and turn left at the sign to Reed's Beach. Continue 1 mile to the bay, then turn right and follow the cottage-lined road to a state parking area. From an observation platform here you will see more birds than you ever imagined existed—if you visit between early May and early June. The timing of peak bird numbers varies from year to year.

Two words of caution: 1) Do not venture onto the beach and disturb the feeding birds; and 2) respect people's private property and do not trespass.

Getting There

Take the Garden State Parkway south to its terminus in Cape May. Then take Lafayette Street (Rte. 633) south to Sunset Boulevard. Turn right onto Sunset and proceed about a mile to the Cape May Migratory Bird Refuge and another mile to Cape May Point State Park.

Facilities: Restrooms and drinking water at Cape May Point State Park. None at Cape May Migratory Bird Refuge or Higbees Beach.

Best Time to Visit: May/June and September/October are best, but any time is good.

For More Information: Contact the Cape May Bird Observatory, 707 E. Lake Drive, Cape May Point, NJ 08212; 609-884-2736.

Nearby Attractions: The Cape May County Zoo is a great, but little-known zoo. And it's free. Watch for signs along the Garden State Parkway. Avoid visiting on weekends between July 4 and Labor Day. The Cape May Observatory (watch for signs on Sunset Boulevard near Cape May Point State Park) has a great bookstore and gift shop and naturalists who can answer any questions that might come up.

About the Authors

SCOTT SHALAWAY holds a Ph.D. in wildlife ecology from Michigan State University and has taught at both Oklahoma State University and the University of Oklahoma. He now makes his living as a freelance writer. His syndicated nature column now reaches more than one million readers each week in more than twenty newspapers, and he writes regularly for several national and regional magazines. He also hosts a weekly radio talk show called *The Wild Side*. This is his fourth book.

Nora Shalaway

L INDA SHALAWAY earned a B.A. in English and journal-ism at the University of Delaware and is now a high school English teacher and freelance writer and editor. She specializes in educational and natural history topics. This is her third book.

The Shalaways grew up in rural Montgomery Coun-ty, Pennsylvania, and now live on a ridge near Cameron, West Virginia. They have two daughters, Nora and Emma.

The Shalaways published their first book with Appalachian Mountain Club Books in 1994, entitled *Quiet Water Canoe Guide: Pennsylvania.*

About the AMC

The Appalachian Mountain Club pursues an active conservation agenda while encouraging responsible recreation. Our philosophy is that successful, long-term conservation depends on firsthand experience of the natural environment. AMC's 71,000 members pursue interests in hiking, canoeing, skiing, walking, rock climbing, bicycling, camping, kayaking, and backpacking, and—at the same time—help safeguard the environment.

Founded in 1876, the club has been at the forefront of the environmental protection movement. As cofounder of several leading New England environmental organizations, and as an active member working in coalition with these and many other groups, the AMC has successfully influenced legislation and public opinion.

Conservation

The most recent efforts in the AMC conservation program include river protection, Northern Forest Lands policy, Sterling Forest (NY) preservation, and support for the Clean Air Act. The AMC depends upon its active members and grassroots supporters to promote this conservation agenda.

Education

The AMC's education department offers members and the general public a wide range of workshops, from introductory camping to the intensive Mountain Leadership School taught on the trails of the White Mountains. In addition, volunteers in each chapter lead hundreds of outdoor activities and excursions and offer introductory instruction in backcountry sports.

Research

The AMC's research department focuses on the forces affecting the ecosystem, including ozone levels, acid rain and fog, climate change, rare flora and habitat protection, and air quality and visibility.

Trails Program

Another facet of the AMC is the trails program, which maintains more than 1,400 miles of trail (including 350 miles of the Appalachian Trail) and more than 50 shelters in the Northeast. Through a coordinated effort of volunteers, seasonal crews, and program staff, the AMC contributes more than 10,000 hours of public service work each summer in the area from Washington, D.C., to Maine.

In addition to supporting our work by becoming an AMC member, hikers can donate time as volunteers. The club offers four unique weekly volunteer base camps in New Hampshire, Maine, Massachusetts, and New York. We also sponsor 10-day service projects throughout the United States, Adopt-a-Trail programs, trails day events, trail skills workshops, and chapter and camp volunteer projects.

The AMC has a long-standing connection to Acadia National Park. Working in cooperation with the National Park Service and Friends of Acadia, the AMC Trails Program provides many opportunities to preserve the park's resources. These include half-day volunteer projects for guests at AMC's Echo Lake Camp, 10-day service projects, weeklong volunteer crews in the fall, and trails day events. For more information on these public-service volunteer opportunities, contact the AMC Trails Program, Pinkham Notch Visitor Center, P.O. Box 298, Gorham NH 03581; 603-466-2721.

Alpine Huts

The club operates eight alpine huts in the White Mountains that provide shelter, bunks and blankets, and hearty meals for hikers. Pinkham Notch Visitor Center, at the foot of Mt. Washington, is base camp to the adventurous and the ideal location for individuals and families new to outdoor recreation. Comfortable bunk rooms, mountain hospitality, and home-cooked, family-style meals make Pinkham Notch Visitor Center a fun and affordable choice for lodging. For reservations, call 603-466-2727.

Publications

At the AMC main office in Boston and at Pinkham Notch Visitor Center in New Hampshire, the bookstore and information center stock the entire line of AMC publications, as well as other trail and river guides, maps, reference materials, and the latest articles on conservation issues. Guidebooks and other AMC gifts are available by mail order (800-262-4455) or by writing AMC, P.O. Box 298, Gorham NH 03581. Also available from the bookstore or by subscription is *Appalachia,* the country's oldest mountaineering and conservation journal.

Alphabetical Listing of Areas